PRAISE FOR DAVID TAYLOR'S *THE NAKED LEADER*

'The One-Minute Manager for a new generation'
Nigel Risner, co-author, *Chicken Soup For The British Soul*

'At last – the antidote to all those wasted "quality" initiatives, there is another way…'
Robin Bloor, Bloor Research Group

'If you are into leadership, then you must be into The Naked Leader. David captures the new spirit of leadership and delivers in a truly inspirational manner'
Rene Carayol, co-author of *Corporate Voodoo*

'The Naked Leader brings fun, adventure and inspiration back into business and personal success'
Adrian Gilpin, Chairman, The Institute of Human Development

'The Naked Leader uses the most advanced techniques available to transform people's ideas about life, without once resorting to jargon, mystery or academic double-speak.'
Joe Crosbie, Head of Marketing, The Children's Society

'The Naked Leader engages everyone, turning dreams into reality.'
Wendy Thorley, IT Director, RSPCA

'The Naked Leader is guaranteed to change the way you think and feel about yourself as a leader'
Gareth Brown, Managing Director, Qube Limited

'This book makes success within everyone's grasp'
Daily Mirror

'At last – a self-help book that is actually helpful'
Computing

'This book delivers again, and again…'
Computer Weekly

D0191830

'The Naked Leader does exactly what it says on the tin'
                                        Business Plus

'The business book bestseller executives are taking on holiday'
                                        Financial Times

the
naked
millionaire

The ultimate fast-track guide to wealth, freedom and fulfilment

David Taylor

CAPSTONE

Library of Congress Cataloguing-in-Publication Data is available

ISBN 9781907312434

A catalogue record for this book is available from the British Library.

Set in 11/13 pt Baskerville by Sparks – www.sparkspublishing.com

Printed in Great Britain by TJ International Ltd, Padstow, Cornwall

This one's for my mum and dad

'Money isn't everything ... but it ranks right up there with oxygen.'

Rita Davenport

(DIS)CLAIMER

This is a work of fact – if and only if you do something with it.

Otherwise, it is a work of fiction.

Legend has it that many years ago, a very special child was born. Unique in natural strengths, talent and personality, this child, from the very moment of birth, knew that it was going to love this thing called 'life'.

The young Child watched and took in the wonders of everything and everyone around it, and so became an Explorer, gaining a reputation for being full of spontaneity and happiness. Soon the Explorer was told that discovery in itself was not enough, and was sent off to school. Hungry for new knowledge, the Explorer became a Student, who gained a reputation for being very learned. However, some of the fun seemed to disappear, somewhere.

Next, the Student was advised that while information was important, it was nothing without real experience. So the Student became a Practitioner, eager to work hard and grow in understanding, and gained a reputation for being worldly wise. However, some of the wonder seemed to fade away, somehow.

And after many years, the Child who had become an Explorer, who became a Student, and then a Practitioner, stopped one day and noticed some things.

That the life it was now living was not so full of everyday joy. That the organization in which it worked was not such a happy place. And that the world in which it lived had so much worry, so much hardship and so much fear. Perhaps there was something about this thing called 'life' that the Practitioner had not yet fully understood.

So the Practitioner set out to understand, and thus became an Adventurer.

All Adventurers need an adventure. To find one, they must apply the formula for guaranteed success: know where you want to go; know where you are now; know what you have to do to get to where you want to go; and do it.

The Adventurer had an idea where it wanted to go – something to do with purpose, happiness and being at peace. It knew where it was, and knew generally what to do, to make its dream, unclear though it was, move closer. The Adventurer had to make things happen, rather than simply let things happen.

This was exciting. However, just as it was about to take its first action, the Adventurer froze in fear, trapped by thoughts and fearful imaginings. It wanted more, but without losing what it already had. More freedom, but not at the expense of safety; more money, but not to the extent of greediness; and, it wanted to be true to itself, yet also connect with others.

And so our Adventurer waited for a sign, a trigger, for something...

And as it waited, a realization dawned. What it once was, it still was. Once a Child, always a Child; once an Explorer, always an Explorer, keen to explore again; once a Student, always a Student, still ready to learn; once a Practitioner, always a Practitioner, still taking in life's rich experiences.

And, from its very first breath, right up to this exact moment, the Adventurer was, still is, and always will be, you.

You have just had a life-changing moment – a sudden dream of what could be. A massive, exciting, personal few seconds of your life – a *'wow'* moment.

You can't wait to share it with someone – you have to or you will simply explode with joy. You want them to share your special feelings too. You run up to them, maybe even grabbing hold of them in your excitement:

'Guess what, I've just had this amazing idea – I think it will make me rich…'

You blurt out your idea, your invention, your dream … you can't get the words out fast enough. And when you have finished, you look at the person in front of you, waiting for the 'well done', the shared joy, the gushing approval.

Hang on – something is wrong. They are not dancing around, or hugging you, or even smiling. They are standing very still, looking at you, as if you are slightly crazy. This in itself reduces your 'amazing idea' to just an 'idea'.

Their next words will show no respect whatsoever: *'With all due respect…'*

Then they put on their boxing gloves, and start to box your dream into submission. After a few hits your 'idea' has been reduced to a silly notion. Each word hits its target: *'You? Keep your feet on the ground… If that was such a good idea don't you think someone else would have done it by now?'* Or *'That's already been done before … ridiculous, impossible, forget it.'*

All because they care about you; perhaps, if it is a parent or partner, because they love you. So much so that they do not want to see you upset and disappointed by going for a dream and then failing. They couldn't handle that.

By now you are on the ropes. Your few weak jabs in reply have no impact. They are coming at you as fast as your dream is becoming the stuff of distant memory. Now they line up the old one-two knockout combination. This person – friend, parent, carer of your soul and sanity – asks you:

One: *'How? How are you going to make this dream come true?'*

You don't know – you only had the idea a few minutes before. You stumble backwards, and whisper rather weakly: *'I don't know.'*

Two: *'Well, if you don't know how, doesn't that give you a clue?'*

And you have had enough – and rather than wait to be hit again, you simply lie down, take the count ... and as for your dream, what was that again?

The countdown
10 THIS BOOK WILL
 9 SHOW YOU EXACTLY
 8 HOW TO
 7 MAKE MONEY
 6 LOTS OF IT
 5 WHILE BEING HAPPY
 4 BY SIMPLY BEING YOURSELF
 3 VERY FAST
 2 NOW GET UP AND START PUNCHING BACK
 1 STARTING WITH YOU AND ME MAKING A DEAL

The Deal: to ensure you get up, every time you are knocked over...

I promise to share with you powerful and specific ways to achieve what you want to achieve, to be happy and fulfilled, while making lots of money and helping others along the way.

And in return:

You promise to take action.

And that action may be what I suggest; or, if you disagree with what I suggest, you will do something else – **but you will do something.**

Whether it is something I suggested, or the complete opposite, that's fine. I do not mind whether you believe in me. I want to know if you believe in *you*.

'If everything seems under control, you're just not going fast enough.'
Mario Andretti, Italian-born American race driver

This is a book about becoming a millionaire – not through investment, although you may invest the money that you make; not through savings, although you will be able to have some of those; and not through betting on the 4.10 pm horse at your local racetrack.

This book is about how to make a million, by being an entrepreneur, and/or by turning yourself or your company into a global brand, and/or by starting and running a successful business.

A fast way to achieve that success is to find someone who has already achieved what you want to achieve, and aim to be like them.

It's a good place to start, but it's not very authentic, and it's not as easy as it sounds – you may know the lyrics to 'Candle in the Wind', but that doesn't make you Elton John.

A faster way to achieve that success is to find someone who has already achieved what you want to achieve, and copy them.

It's a great place to start. Some call it modelling. But it does have one significant downfall: everyone makes mistakes, gets things wrong and takes longer to achieve something than they could. If you decide to copy them, you will probably also copy their mistakes. If you decided to model Martha Stewart, your muffins would rise, you would know what to do with pumpkin seeds – and you might also serve five months in prison.

The fastest way to achieve that success is to find someone who has already achieved what you want to achieve, and copy them, but avoiding the same mistakes that they made along the way – or at the very least knowing what they are going to be, so you are well positioned to overcome them, jump over them or go around them.

I am just an ordinary guy, who has had the great fortune to work with, observe and learn from, scores of companies, hundreds of entrepreneurs and thousands of leaders from across all walks of life, from all around the world.

This book is written with some insight, sure, but it comes much more from an unending stream of hindsight. After all, I have made my own mistakes:

- I have embarrassed my own daughter in a talk at her school so badly that she didn't talk to me for several weeks, and pleaded with me never to go back again. When I did, she threatened not to attend. Thankfully she did, though, and I put it right.
- I am one of a very, very small circle of authors who had a book deal 'in the bag' with one of the top publishers in the world – signed and sealed, and all I had to do was deliver. I delivered something – how shall I put it? Not very good! By that stage my head was so big I couldn't get through doors and I learned a huge lesson, which I will share with you.
- And, the one which I am most embarrassed about: I was chairman of a football club – my beloved local team, Woking – in the season we were relegated, largely because I led the recruitment team that chose the wrong manager. You may wonder what this story is doing in a book on being a successful entrepreneur. For me, it certainly fast-tracked my ability to handle failure and get back up again – I have learned so much and continue to be involved, to help make it right. Also, it was a hobby that got out of control and threatened our business, and my health. Most of all, it helped me learn how to deal with detractors, something you will have to master too. I will help you do that, even when you may agree with them!

This is probably the most scary, personal 'How To' book that I have written. However, contrary to what many authors will tell you, books are not written for the authors themselves, they are written for their readers.

Like the other 'Naked' books, this is your book, not mine.

The Naked Millionaire is organized so as to give you choices on how you read it, and in which order you make happen what you read.

- *Journey Zero – Fast-track it and read only the most essential parts.* And don't feel guilty, I won't be offended!
- *Journey One – Front to back – Start at the beginning, keep reading and taking action, until you get to the end, and then stop (reading, that is).* The most 'logical', structured way to read it.
- *Journey Two – The Journey of Hindsight.* This is the journey I wish, in hindsight, I had taken. This is my recommended journey, as you will achieve success faster than I did.
- *Journey Three – The Journey of Misadventure.* This is the journey of lessons learned – the journey I took. To share with you the mistakes I made, so you avoid them.

Plus, of course, you have three more choices of your own:

- Read the book as you wish.
- Read by dipping in and out.
- Or don't read it at all.

That last one may sound a bit crazy, as you are already reading it! When it comes to business books, we live in a crazy world. Most people go through the following process – see book, buy book, carry book around, place next to bed (where you hope the contents of the book somehow transfer by osmosis) and at some stage file alongside all the other (still-to-be-read) books on your shelf.

And the main reason for this is: *You don't actually want to read this book – you want to achieve any benefits it has to offer you – and you want to make them happen, very fast.*

In fact, in many ways, reading a book is a complete nuisance, holding you up from achieving what you want to achieve. Sorry to keep you.

Read it as you wish; after all, you will have the choice at the end of each action, to jump across to a different journey.

Just, please, one simple plea directly from the book, itself: Please, please, however you read me – *do something*.

The single difference between people who achieve success, by their own definition, and in all walks of life, and those who don't, is that successful people take action – they actually *do something*.

It doesn't matter how you read this book, it only matters what you choose to do. Not me, not another reader, but *you*.

This is where we come to the true classification of this book. Most bookshops will locate it under 'Business' or 'Entrepreneurship' or 'Leadership'. Actually, this book is ultimately none of those things. It is really a 'whodunnit?'.

You know that dream you had a few years ago? The one that, for whatever reason, you did not pursue, only for someone else to make it happen. Whodunnit? Theydunnit!

You know that dream you have right now? To be free, to be yourself, to help others in the world with the skills that you have – the things that will combine to make you very wealthy?

What are you, personally, going to do about it?

Someone will – someone reading this will take action.

Will it be you?

So that in years to come the world will know – Youdunnit!

And as you do, make sure you record your achievements, your challenges, your moments of 'Wow!', so that you can share them with others; so that you can help others; so you can write the story of your life, and what you did, perhaps to pass on through the generations of your family.

> *'"Thou shalt not" is soon forgotten, but "once upon a time" will last forever.'*
>
> Philip Pullman

This idea that you can achieve so much may make you feel uncomfortable. You may think that such thoughts are arrogant, or big-headed.

In that case, may I ask that we go forward from here on a level playing field?

I want you to consider the possibility that you don't have the skills, strengths and talent that you need to achieve your dream. That is a very real possibility – after all, there are plenty of people who will tell you that.

Just as long as you also consider the possibility that you *do have* the skills, strengths and talent...

> *'Do not let what you cannot do interfere with what you can.'*
> John Wooden, college basketball coach, who won 10 championships in 12 years

Your book – your choice

The book is structured into seven sections:

I   Your Self: Be an Authentic Millionaire
II   Your Brand: Design a Global Brand
III   Your Business: Start and Grow Your Business
IV   Your Warning! Avoid the Pitfalls that I Didn't
V   Your Secrets: See What Others Don't
VI   Your Speaking: Present as a Professional Speaker
VII Your Book: Write a Bestseller

Within each section are three chapters, giving twenty-one chapters in total.

If you choose one of the 'moving about' journeys (Two – Hindsight or Three – Misadventure) you will cover all chapters in different orders. At the end of each chapter is a signpost to the next chapter on your chosen journey.

The book ends (at the back!) with a case study on the company 'onebestway' as featured and turned around in the Virgin One TV programme *The Naked Office*. Finally, there is a list of resources to help keep your success sustainable.

Each journey starts on page 3 with Chapter 1, Simply Be Yourself (It's all you need to be). The only place you can ever begin is with yourself. Many millionaires say that all that happened was they started in the right place, at the right time.

Well, the right place is wherever you are, right now, and the right time is now.

CONTENTS

JOURNEY ONE – FRONT TO BACK

JOURNEY TWO – THE JOURNEY OF HINDSIGHT

CONTENTS

JOURNEY THREE – THE JOURNEY OF MISADVENTURE

YOUR SELF – BE AN AUTHENTIC MILLIONAIRE

'In the 21ˢᵗ Century, the real leaders will be the people with a unique personality, skill or product. And uniqueness never drops out of committees; it arises from deep within a person, from your essential self.'
Martha Beck *– Finding your own North Star*

SUMMARY

Be clear on what you want to achieve, take ownership for everything that you do and say, and also for the talents that you already have, especially those you were born with. Make a true decision on what you are going to do, and then do it. As you do, help others, always over-deliver to customers and be persistently persistent. Then, and only then, will you find that perfect balance between happiness, wealth creation, and making a difference to yourself, others and the world.

The Naked Leader is you, not me, and the message is blindingly obvious.

It is entirely built on common sense, the stuff you already know, deep down. And, deep down, you already know that your future is your choice, and no-one else's: as an individual, as a team or as an organization.

If you believe that, you are making a choice. If you do not believe that, you are also making a choice. After all, there are people out there in exactly the same, or worse, circumstances than you, who have gone on to achieve what you want to achieve, and more.

The single difference between people who achieve success and those who don't is **action**.

What you actually do – how you act, and react – is everything. It doesn't matter what you know, it doesn't really matter what you say; your results always come down to one thing and one thing alone: what you do. What you, your people and your organization actually do, each and every day. Everything else is just noise.

If you want success (by your own definition) in any area of your life, know what you want to achieve. Know your desired outcome, take ownership, make a true decision, and then do something. And ask yourself the ultimate question of success:

Does what I am doing take me/us closer to achieving my/our desired outcome, or not?

If it does, do more of the same; if it does not, do something else – and keep going until you achieve what you want, or choose to give up.

And, to remove any fear, simply remember that one day you will close your eyes and you will die. So, get with the programme. Live life to the full, while you can, or don't – your choice.

WHY NAKED?

Many others will tell you to be more than what you have become. Many people will inspire you to be the very best that you can be. I invite you to be the very best that you already are.

On the day you were born, naked, you had everything you needed, to be anything you want. On the day that you die, naked, you will look back on whether you achieved everything that you could have. If all of this comes down to one thing, it is about fulfilling the promise of your first few seconds, while ensuring no regrets in your last...

Your truth, integrity and authenticity come from deep within, and your success will come from removing false, limiting beliefs that separate you from the essence of who you truly are, and always have been. It is this separation, from what you feel now to who you truly

4

are, that is the root cause of many anxieties, worries and fears. When you accept that, then you start to move towards your major premise – your underlying belief system. Just reading this, and believing whatever you believe, is sometimes enough to bring you an inner peace and joy that reconnects you with your inner power.

Sustained success does not happen by accident or by chance. It happens as a result of a specific process, an exact formula.

THE FORMULA FOR GUARANTEED SUCCESS

Tell everyone you know, destroy the mystery and hype surrounding business success, and personal leadership, forever.

1 Know where you want to go/be – the *what* – (dreams and outcomes). Have massive dreams or, at the very least, set a standard for yourself that is higher than anyone else can ever reasonably expect of you. Focus on what you want – not what you don't want.
2 Know where you are now – the *you* – (ownership and honesty). Take ownership of everything that you say and do. Never say anything behind your close colleagues' backs that you would not say to their faces. Always raise issues when they need to be raised.
3 Know what you have to do, to get to where you want to be – the *moment* – (choices and true decisions). From the moment you are born, until the moment that you die, you will only ever do something to the best of your ability for one reason and one reason alone, and that is because *you want to* – because you choose to. When you make a decision, make it 'true' – i.e. you will actually carry it through. It only takes a single heartbeat to make such a decision.
4 Do it! – the first action – the *how* – (action and persistence). Take one action. Then ask yourself: Does this action, this behaviour, this thought, take me closer to where I want to go, or closer to who I want to be? In other words, does it serve or help me, our team, or our organization, or does it not?

If 'Yes', do more of the same...

If 'No', then do something else, and if that doesn't 'work' then...

Please put the next page on a wall where you can see it every day.

Do something else…

And if that doesn't work, then do something else.
And if that doesn't work, then do something else.
And if that doesn't work, then do something else.
And if that doesn't work, then do something else.
And if that doesn't work, then do something else.
And if that doesn't work, then do something else.
And if that doesn't work, then do something else.
And if that doesn't work, then do something else.
And if that doesn't work, then do something else.
And if that doesn't work, then do something else.
And if that doesn't work, then do something else.
And if that doesn't work, then do something else.
And if that doesn't work, then do something else.
And if that doesn't work, then do something else.
And if that doesn't work, then do something else.

And if that doesn't work, *then do something else.*
And if that doesn't work, *then do something else.*
And if that doesn't work, *then do something else.*
And if that doesn't work, *then do something else.*

Or give up.

If you ever feel like giving up, remember that you will never know whether, if you had just kept going for a bit longer, then you might have moved forward. Many entrepreneurs believe that it is at the moment of your biggest despair that you come closest to the moment of your biggest breakthrough. If you give up, you will never know, but you will always wonder…

Your reaction

Your reaction to what you have just read will have everything to do with whether or not you are going to complete your adventure, and become a Naked Millionaire.

You may find this message – be the very best that you already are – an inspiring one. Great. Thank you for being inspired. However, please know this: I really don't care.

Inspiration is simply not a strategy. It's what you do with that inspiration that really matters.

I don't want to know how you feel about what I write, or say – I want to know what you personally are going to *do*.

Or, when you hear this message – be the very best that you already are – it may make you feel rather sceptical, or even cynical. Great. Thank you for being sceptical, or even cynical. However, please know this: I really don't care.

Being sceptical or cynical is simply not a strategy. It's what you do with those feelings that really matters.

I don't want to know how you feel about what I write, or say. I want to know what you personally are going to *do*.

When you hear this message – be the very best that you already are – it may make you feel very open-minded – in other words, you believe it may be true, or it may not. You are open to both possibilities. Great. Thank you for being so open-minded. However, please know this: I really don't care.

While being open-minded may sound good, it is simply not a strategy. It's what you do with your open mind that really matters.

I don't want to know how you feel about what I write, or say. I want to know what you personally are going to *do*.

What you feel will determine what you believe – or it will, if you let it. What you believe will determine what you do – or it will, if you let it. Your adventure towards being a Naked Millionaire, towards achieving anything in your life, in your career or in your organization, will come down to one thing and one thing alone: what you do. What you personally do, each and every day, in each and every moment – starting right now.

Whether or not you succeed on your own personal journey will also come down to how much you *want* to succeed.

THE KILLER QUESTION

If it's all so simple, why isn't everyone doing it?

1   'Simple' does not equal 'easy'. Indeed, 'simple' is often dismissed or looked down on, by jargon-speaking academics, expensive consultants and highbrow media.
2   Because 'common sense' has become not so common.
3   It can be hard to simply be yourself. At work, or when starting a company, we can feel the need to conform, or seek a compromise view. I am not saying these things are 'right' or 'wrong', but conformity and compromise won't help you on this adventure.
4   And the biggest of them all – you went through childhood.

> *'We're born to win, but programmed to fail! We are programmed into the negative from the moment we come into this world. It starts with our upbringing. By the time you reach the age of 18, you've heard the word 'no' 200,000 times, seen 30,000 acts of violence, and have received more than 12 million messages in the form of advertising telling you how to look, what to eat, and how to feel. No wonder most of us grow up with a negative self-image!'*
> Desi Williamson – *Get Off Your Assets! How to Unleash the Power in You*

Think, just for a moment: at home, how often did you hear the word 'no' when you were a child? At school, how often you were taught what to think, rather than how to think? How many 'rules' did you learn at a young age?

'Speak when you are spoken to.' (Great advice for communication.)

'Children should be seen and not heard.' (Know your place.)

'Don't talk to strangers.' (Best avoid a career in selling.)

Loving 'no' is the only way to meet that 'yes' that is just around the corner.

As a Naked Millionaire, you must reverse this teaching. The very best salespeople, entrepreneurs and business people learn to love the word 'no'. This sets them apart from their competitors – making that next sales call, sending their book off again after many rejections, taking on board all the feedback you will receive without being hurt, or taking it personally…

CHOOSE YOUR BELIEFS WITH CARE

We start to form our beliefs when we are young. We form beliefs from listening to our parents, teachers, friends and family. And these beliefs (such as which football team is best!) can have an extraordinary power and stay with us for the rest of our lives.

How many of the following 'facts' or beliefs do you still hold as true?

There are seven colours in a rainbow.

There are as many colours in the rainbow as the eye can see. Rainbows, like sunlight, contain a continuous spectrum that does not neatly divide into red, orange, yellow, green, blue, indigo and violet.

The Great Wall of China is the only man-made object visible from the moon.

The only thing you can see from the moon is a beautiful sphere, mostly white (clouds), some blue (ocean), patches of yellow (deserts), and every once in a while some green vegetation. No man-made object is visible on this scale.

If you don't know it now, you will never know it.

Often told to students just before they sit an exam – absolute rubbish! Our short-term memories serve us well in recalling what we have just taken in (the same applies for meeting notes, shopping lists and the key points of the talk you are about to make at an event).

You are not enough.

No matter what your age, your knowledge or experience, you all no doubt have been told many times that 'you are clever' or 'you are stupid' or 'you are good' or 'you are bad'. These comments are *always* – just someone else's opinion. The only fact, the only indisputable fact, is that you are. Full stop. As you read that again – 'you are', and you think about what that means for you, it may be that you are feeling a little more excited about your journey ahead.

I was once told by a 'teacher' at school that I had 'something missing'. Rosaleen Moriarty-Simmonds changed my belief in this forever. Because she most certainly does have something missing: as a result of her mother being prescribed thalidomide during pregnancy, Rosaleen has no arms or legs (just four fingers, two sprouting from each shoulder and thirteen toes on legs which come to an abrupt end above the knee.) And yet, she knows she has nothing 'missing' at all...

Anyone can achieve

Being determined to succeed is crucial. Born in 1960 as one of the generation of thalidomide children, I learned determination very quickly.

I knew the key to my future was a good education, and so, despite being 'written off' as an academic failure, I secured good 'O' level grades, obtained a diploma in Business Studies and gained an Honours Degree in Psychology.

Life is not always a bed of roses. Successes will be matched by an equal number of disappointments.

Opportunities only present themselves. Never say 'never'; have fun and work with passion to accomplish achievable goals.

If I can do it with just four fingers and thirteen toes, then anyone can!

Reproduced by permission of Rosaleen Moriarty-Simmonds
(www.rms-consultancy.co.uk)

YOUR THREE KEY ACTIONS

- Be clear on the exact outcomes, the results that you want.
- Take personal ownership and accountability for everything that you say and do – there is nothing 'wrong' with you.
- Make a true decision – decide to go for what you want and that you will settle for nothing less, then take one action on your journey. If it takes you closer to where you want to go, do more of the same. If not, then do something else, and so on until you succeed. What you do is all.

If you choose to continue on Journey One, Front to Back, keep on reading and I won't insult your intelligence again!

The Journey of Hindsight continues at IV Your Warning! – 10 How to Make the Big Decision (Don't give up your day job, just yet) on page 131.

The Journey of Misadventure continues at VII Your Book – 19 How to Begin Writing a Book (and finish it!) on page 231.

2   GET READY FOR THE (BUMPY) RIDE AHEAD

'Little minds are tamed and subdued by misfortune, but great minds rise above them.'

Washington Irving

SUMMARY
Your journey to being a Naked Millionaire will be a bumpy one. You will face many challenges and it will be tough. Stay true to yourself. Enjoy your journey as you learn more about yourself. Do what needs to be done, when it needs to be done, and that involves hard work, focus and discipline.

Are you sitting comfortably?

Good.

Then I won't begin.

This book is not about being 'comfortable' – this book is about being different from other people – different in three main ways:

1   *Taking ownership* of your future, and of your life – you will not expect someone else to do it for you, and you will not blame other people when things do not go as you would like them to.
2   *Doing what needs to be done*, when and how it needs to be done. That is likely to involve hard work, often when you least feel like doing it.
3   *Being confident* – you believe that you have the skills and talent to be a Naked Millionaire. And just as you never need to shout about it, so you will never believe anyone who tells you that your skills and talent are not enough.

Are you up for it? Are you prepared to go on a journey very much less travelled? Are you prepared to be one of the few, and not one of the many?

If you are feeling comfortable, then you may not yet be ready for your adventure, to make your idea a reality, build your business and turn your money into real wealth.

OWNERSHIP

'If it is to be, it is up to me.'

William H. Johnsen

(Born with his head much smaller than his body and nicknamed Zip the Pinhead, William used his deformity to his advantage by becoming a top freak-show artist.)

To achieve success, William did what successful people do – he took personal ownership, accountability and responsibility for everything he did. That is how he acted, and how he reacted.

And that is the uncomfortable part: everyone would have to agree at some level that they have total and absolute control over how they act, what they say and do.

Very few will accept that they have total and absolute control over how they react – to what others say, and do. To the weather. To that traffic jam. To this circumstance and that. With absolutely no blame.

If you arrive an hour late for a meeting, that is your responsibility. The fact the trains were delayed is irrelevant.

If you make a mistake in a presentation, admit it.

And if you cannot deliver something on time, say so and apologize in advance as soon as you realize the situation.

Just by taking ownership, you will be joining a select few people in this world.

Now, to make it even fewer...

DOING WHAT NEEDS TO BE DONE

'There is always room for those who can be relied upon to deliver the goods when they say they will.'

Napoleon Hill, www.naphill.org

Imagine the scene. It is after 10 pm and you have just got back home after a really tough day. You have not eaten a proper meal, you are tired and you have an early start tomorrow.

You go straight to bed, and just as you are about to sleep, you suddenly remember that you made a promise to write an article for a magazine, and that you would send it through by the end of today.

You glance at the clock – 10.30 pm – and a little voice in your head tells you: 'That's OK, get up early and send it in the morning. You write better in the morning anyway, and as long as it gets to them by 9 am it will be fine. Now, go to sleep.'

What do you do? Do you (a) Go to sleep; or (b) Throw back the covers, go write the article, and send it through?

The answer all depends on how you feel – if you're up to it, then throw back the covers, throw cold water in your face and go write and send the article.

If, on the other hand, you do not feel up to it, then throw back the covers, throw cold water in your face and go write and send the article.

This is not a book that says you must 'go the extra mile' or talks about how horse races are won by an inch and no-one ever remembers second place.

It is a book that says this – if you commit to do something, do it.

CONFIDENCE

'I quit being afraid when my first venture failed and the sky didn't fall down.'

Allen H. Neuharth
(Neuharth experienced many failures and setbacks,
including bankruptcy, on his road to being the founder
of *USA Today*.)

Confidence is absolutely critical to your success, in running a successful business, in forming trusted relationships and in becoming a Naked Millionaire.

That's confidence, not arrogance. The two are very different – confidence is knowing you have abilities; arrogance is shouting about them.

Arrogant people tell others how well they are doing (when they are probably not; they are simply feeding their own need to be superior). Confident people don't need to tell anyone how well they are doing (they already know). As a confident person, you are likely to show humility, help other people on your journey, and be modest about your achievements.

The fastest way to be confident? Act as if you are confident. The mind cannot tell the difference between something that happens in reality and something it imagines with emotional intensity. So, literally, pretend that you are confident and act as you would if you really were, and you will be. As you feel more confident, so some existing beliefs that do not help you achieve success will crumble.

I have been told there are no new ideas to be had (I believed this for two years, during which time I never once had a new idea!); I have been told that you need certain qualifications to be successful (you don't); and I suppose the biggest 'rule' I was taught when I was younger was that my success was 'just around the corner'. I have been looking for it everywhere, and have yet to find it. Because it is nowhere, except sometimes in my own mind.

I will coach you on exactly how to break these rules. How to smash them into smithereens, and write some new ones of your own that are useful and meaningful.

Tuesday 13 January 2004, Elstree, London. I had been presenting to a group of entrepreneurs. It had been an exciting evening, with such a positive, can-do attitude in the room, and time just flew by, so much so that I missed my last train home. One of the delegates kindly offered me a lift home and we walked together to his car – to his Rolls-Royce, to be more precise.

During the journey I complimented him on his car, and after a while I plucked up the courage to say: 'I hope you don't mind my asking – did you make your money before you came, or here?'

His reply was clear: 'Here.'

His follow-up comment was surprising: 'This is the best country in the world to be an entrepreneur, the best country by far.'

Long pause – more M25, me thinking about the negative press we have in Britain and the very negative attitude towards people who make money through their own hard work (as opposed to those who win it in a lottery). I expressed this sentiment, by now hanging on this guy's every word. This 'guy' who had attended one of my talks on how to be successful, who was driving a beautiful black Rolls-Royce, and who was driving over 120 miles out of his way just to take me home, at 1.30 in the morning.

He said: 'The reasons you talk about are the very reasons why this is the best country to go for it.'

'How so?' I asked.

And, in the course of this entire book, and your new exciting adventure, please always remember his reply. Without taking his eyes off the road ahead, he said matter-of-factly:

'People get so put off by those things, they are scared – scared to be themselves, scared to have an idea and very scared to start a business. So, those that decide to do something, despite feeling very scared, cannot fail.'

Are you sitting uncomfortably?

Excellent.

Then we will begin…

YOUR THREE KEY ACTIONS

- Get out of your comfort zone, and get out of it right now.
- Feel positive towards money and the prospect of being happy.
- The more uncomfortable you feel, the readier you are.

The Journey of Hindsight continues at 3 How to Form Key Relationships (People and money) on page 20.

The Journey of Misadventure continues at VII Your Book – 20 How to Have It Published (while staying sane) on page 251.

3

HOW TO FORM KEY RELATIONSHIPS
(PEOPLE AND MONEY)

'Life is an echo. What you send out – you get back. What you give – you get.'

Zig Ziglar

SUMMARY
Form trusted relationships with people, follow through and then *get paid*. Be nice to people you do not have to be nice to. When you fall out with a business colleague do something about it, early. Have a relationship with money that attracts it into your life – i.e. value it as energy, a symbol of success. You can be happy, have money and make a difference to others.

Your success in becoming a Naked Millionaire will come down to your ability to build trusted relationships.

Let me put that another way, so there can be absolutely no doubt in your mind, or on your adventure: If you want to have no money, your success in achieving this will come down to your *inability* to build trusted relationships.

Before we come to relationships with people, there is the small matter of your relationship with ... eh, sorry, I am about to write that politically incorrect word that we don't talk about in polite society – a word that can make us feel very comfortable, selfish and greedy.

Ladies and gentlemen, I give you:

MONEY

As you embark on your 'selfish' journey to being filthy rich, not content with your roots or what you have right now, always remember that the best things in life are free. And remember that when you make money, others will think you must have broken the law in some way, unless you win the lottery, in which case that's OK.

Considering money has been around a while, many people still have huge hang-ups about it. Money is the last great taboo! We can swear, smoke, drink alcohol, make open jokes about sex, and yet, when it comes to money, especially being rich – that's a no-go area.

In many countries in the world today, it is more socially acceptable (and tax-free) to win the lottery than it is to work hard (and pay tax). There are many reasons for this, and why so many people have an unhappy, unhelpful and unhealthy relationship with money. Every day we read about people who are rich and unhappy. So much so, that some people have actually introduced a 'rule' that you can't be financially successful AND happy! Just because they don't have both, they don't believe that anyone else can, either.

You will often hear the expression 'money doesn't matter'.

Yeah, right. Go pay your mortgage with happiness, or love. 'Hey, I am a bit short this month, how about a hug instead?'

Anyone who thinks or says that money doesn't matter has usually got very little of it.

Other people's relationships with money do not matter right now; what matters is **your** relationship with money.

I assume that, because you are reading this, you have a desire to make money. Great, let's remove any final taboos you may have about being wealthy:

Rich is selfish.

Which is more 'selfish', to take ownership of your life and make your own way, or to be constantly dependent on others? Besides, have you ever known a poor philanthropist?

It's disgusting to be 'filthy rich'.

Now this is just silly, because with money, you are more likely to be able to buy soap, shampoo and hot water.

Being rich means you're not content with your roots.

'Research by Dr Mark Taylor in the UK, shows that people's wellbeing is "strongly linked" to their financial capability.' Britain in 2010 – published by the Economic and Social Research Council

You may be perfectly 'content' with your roots; however, you have simply decided to grow a bigger, stronger tree that will last long after you have died.

Money can't buy you happiness.

Are you more likely to be able to have freedom in your life with money, or without? Why don't you get money and then decide for yourself?

'Research by Dr Mark Taylor in the UK, shows that people's wellbeing is "strongly linked" to their financial capability.' *Britain in 2010* – published by the Economic and Social Research Council

The best things in life are free.

Absolutely, fresh air, love and … I can't think of anything else that could possibly fall into this category. No more shelter, warmth, clothing, food, entertainment, holidays, travel – yes, I am exaggerating to make a point, simply because this quote so often translates to *the only things you really need in life are free*.

Isn't it amazing that so many people perpetuate this unhelpful relationship with money? Because if you have a helpful relationship with money (one taking you closer to achieving what you really want) you are truly one of the few, and not one of the many. And being one of the few is absolutely critical to being a Naked Millionaire.

If anyone says something negative to you about the journey you are on, be gentle with them, and simply ask yourself – are they on this journey, or are you?

In a similar vein, a critical question for you is this: are you jealous of people who have more money than you?

Yes? Remember this: their success is not your failure, unless you let it be so.

No? Fantastic. There is plenty of money to go around.

Let's get back to basics

What is money? Money is money. Meaning? Whatever you want it to mean. And that's it.

To me, money is simply a tool used to transact the exchange of goods and services between people.

To other entrepreneurs, it has been described as 'energy'.

What is it to you?

That is your choice. Choose wisely, if you want to continue your journey forward, and most certainly if, right now, your starting point is having a nasty gap in your economy.

How to be a money magnet

Ten powerful ways to attract money:

1 Be generous: help others less fortunate than yourself.

2 Be grateful for the money that you have, no matter how much or how little that may be, and value money: if you see a penny in the street, pick it up.

3 Do not be jealous of other people who have money – their success is not your failure. Be pleased for them.

4 Do not feel guilty about having money – feeling guilty actually repels wealth and keeps it away from you because you will do everything you can to avoid pain (and if money gives you pain...).

5 Be passionate about everything you do. Surround yourself with people who are similarly passionate.

6 If you lose money, don't play the victim. Learn from what has happened, and be grateful for the lesson.

7 Always keep your promises – say what you mean and mean what you say.

8 Expect to be wealthy – it is inevitable. That is wealth attraction.

9 Believe in abundance. There is plenty of money around in the world.

10 Always be true to yourself and totally authentic.

PEOPLE

How to build a trusted relationship with yourself

No matter how logical we think we are, or we appear to be, deep down we are all living, breathing bundles of emotional energy.

You will never, *never*, be able to build a totally trusted relationship with any other human being, until you can build such a trusted relationship with yourself.

That is because, unless you trust yourself, and all that you think, say and do, you will always be seeking the approval of others – asking their permission before you feel confident in taking action. I believe this is the single biggest disabler to taking action: waiting for someone else, or indeed for ourselves, to give us that permission.

What if it never comes?

At best, we stay in the comfortable life that we have, always wondering if there is something more; at worst, we freeze into inaction.

This important theme is covered at various points in the book, to make sure it gets you at least once, no matter which journey you take.

Naked Millionaires don't need anyone's permission except their own.

There is just one exception here. If you are married with children, i.e. you have people who are dependent on you, it is a very good idea to share your thoughts, plans and ambition with them. After all, life for you, and for those whose lives you touch, is about to change forever.

Seeking approval is the surest way not to find it (how ironic is that?).

That proviso aside, this permission thing hits people from all angles, every moment of every day.

You will need to break free from seeking approval of others, and from their opinions, judgements and adherence to conformity. When you decide to go for things, expect other people – often complete strangers to you – to attack you. They will shout from the online rooftops that you have no 'right' to do this. What they really mean is that they don't have the bravery to do it for themselves, and so why should you? Accept in advance that this will happen, and celebrate it when it does!

You will never become a well-respected person and brand without detractors and naysayers, and these people may be very vocal in their opposition to you. You need that; you need these people talking about you, having a go at what you have done, to get known, create debate and change things.

Inertia seems to come to the fore in challenging economic times. Inside organizations, people are scared about losing their jobs, and so they do not take any risks. They don't do anything unless they have the clear and unequivocal permission from their boss or peers that it is okay. They hold on to as much information and as many skills as they can; after all, the route to job security is to make yourself totally and absolutely indispensable, right?

What a myth – that is the very fast route to being got rid of!

In all times, especially tough ones, organizations (other people around you) need people who go for it, who take initiatives, and above all do something.

Oh, the irony of all those organizations, worldwide, who spend so much money on risk analysis, and yet couldn't take a risk if their lives depended on it.

If you think that waiting for another's permission or indeed waiting for anything will help you to become a millionaire, then think again. No, actually, wait.

That's right – stop reading, right now, and wait.

Waiting for permission simply makes you wait.

Besides, – 'Patience is a virtue' and 'All good things come to those who wait'.

Now, your waiting can stop, because *you have permission*.

To have a dream.

To take action in achieving your dream.

Now.

People you meet every day in the course of life

'You can always tell someone's character by the way they treat those they don't need to treat well.'
Mission Impossible 3 – by Alex Kurtzman, Roberto Orci and J.J. Abrams

Have you noticed how differently people treat other people, because of status and importance? Of course you have; that is at the root of our celebrity culture.

In addition, we all know that it is important, for all sorts of reasons, to be 'nice' to your partner, your family and friends, your boss, your boss's boss, and so on.

What some people know, and that 'some' now includes you, is how critical it is to be 'nice' to – i.e. to treat with courtesy and respect – people you do not stand to gain from immediately and obviously.

These include the waiter serving you at a business lunch (and observe how others treat him/her; it tells you something about their true character), the bus or taxi driver, that tourist who stops you and asks you for directions when you are already running late for a meeting.

And more, far more.

Receptionists, cleaners, chauffeurs, and most of all, personal assistants (PAs).

Receptionists know people, cleaners overhear gossip, chauffeurs know more about a company overall than anyone else does, and PAs are the most powerful group of people in any organization – because they look after the diary – the time – of their bosses.

How to build a trusted relationship with others

You will never become a millionaire on your own. You will only achieve this with the help, advice, support, custom, business and money of other people.

And now you have that trust in yourself, you can build that trust in, and from, others.

Trust is very different from 'approval' or 'permission' – trust gives you freedom.

The first three seconds

When we meet someone new, we decide whether we 'like' them in less than three seconds. We have to like someone if we are to trust them later. At a deeply powerful subconscious level, we like people who are similar to ourselves. Indifferent or negative first impressions can be very difficult to turn around.

How do you build rapport in those first few moments?

Shaking hands

1   Make sure you don't have a sweaty or sticky hand. Be prepared if you know introductions are forthcoming.
2   Make eye contact and smile – make it a genuine smile. Do not smile straight away; delay by a tenth of a second after eye contact (any quicker seems false). Also, smile with your mouth and your eyes. Be genuinely happy to meet *all* new people.
3   Introduce yourself. Extend your right hand and grip their right hand. Not too strong a grip and not too weak. Imaging you are holding an egg – you don't want to crush it and you don't want to drop it!
4   Shake hands, once or twice from the elbow (the wrist is too limp and the shoulder too strong).
5   Greet warmly and, if you had difficulty catching their name, get them to repeat it and, if it is very unfamiliar and you still

can't catch it, ask them to spell it. This will impress them, because if it is difficult to pick up, others will have found the same and not had the gumption to persist with finding out what it is. And really, their name is very important to them.

6   Don't wipe your hand straight afterwards even if their hand was sweaty. Wait until they are out of sight.

Starting the conversation

To open dialogue, ask them a question about themselves and start to mirror (match and pace) their body language and voice. If you are interested in learning more about these techniques please visit www.nakedleader.com for information on appropriate workshops, resources and events.

People like to talk about themselves especially if you seem interested in them, and you should be; there are so many interesting people out there to meet.

Practise the above with your partner and friends; have a stock of questions that are ready in your head for when you meet people.

And remember our Deal: you will do what I suggest or you will do something else, but you will not do nothing.

So, if you do not believe what I suggest will help you build rapport then do the opposite: stand with a surly look, don't offer your hand and don't attempt to say anything – that should do the trick!

Your three seconds, your choice.

Your three seconds, on which much of your business and wealth will depend. Because, as we discuss elsewhere on your adventure, the majority of your business – sales, income, money – will come from people you know, people who already trust you.

Your key trusted business relationships are with:

- existing clients/customers
- potential clients/customers
- your business partners/staff/co-workers

We will cover the first two of these in more detail in the Your Business chapters. For now, let's look at your relationship with your business partners and staff.

When you start your business, you may need funding to get it off the ground. This may bring in other people and directors, who may also have part-ownership of the business or company.

Your relationship with these fellow directors/business partners is absolutely critical to your success, and the time to get it right is at the very beginning, when all looks fine and rosy.

The main reason new companies fail, often before they have started, comes down to relationships going wrong.

Many books will tell you that such relationships most often 'go wrong' because of different opinions about how the company goes forward. I do not agree with that.

I believe that such relationships most often 'go wrong' because people do not discuss, debate and resolve their different opinions about how the company goes forward.

It is absolutely critical to have 'different opinions' – it is equally as important to discuss, debate and decide on having one way forward, which everyone buys into.

You must have this openness, healthy debate and agreement about the way forward in order to encourage people to speak their minds more openly, and, perhaps surprisingly, to encourage people to have more ideas of their own. One of these may well be the breakthrough you need as a business.

To achieve this, take these three actions in your company, of whatever size:

1 Ensure that people know they are encouraged to speak their opinion, and will be listened to, provided it is constructive. (You need robust discussions, different perspectives and ideas.)
2 Make sure that everyone knows whom to go to, and where to go, to find out information and that they can do this without fear or favour.
3 Be a role model. Treat others as you wish to be treated and create a culture of cooperation and openness.

A large number of companies fail because of director fallouts.

These are most often about one of the following:

• Unclear intellectual property – who owns the 'rights' to the name of the company or product, or the idea?
• Confusing roles and responsibilities – make sure everyone in the company has a clear role, knows how what they are doing helps achieve the aims of the organization. Apply this to everyone, including people working from home.
• Personality fallout – you no longer 'like' one another. Get over it and grow up. You don't have to 'like' one another, but you do have to respect one another.

To help resolve these issues, on the next page is a 'code of conduct' to use as a starting point in any joint venture.

Use it and amend it as you wish, get everyone's thoughts and input, discuss and agree the final document and then have everyone sign it as a pledge of their personal commitment.

Note, this is not a legally binding contract, and it is not intended to be. If people start to make reference to lawyers and legal recourse, you need to go forward to mediation, arbitration or separation.

OUR AGREEMENT

1 What unites us is more powerful than anything that may threaten to separate us.

2 We have a clear outcome – a specific result that will become the cornerstone on which we are all agreed. We are all totally committed to achieving that.

3 Intellectual property, i.e. who owns what ideas, is clear from the beginning.

4 We all have clear roles in how we achieve that outcome. These roles must overlap if we are to be successful, and when that overlap becomes an issue we will resolve it.

5 We respect, welcome and celebrate our similarities and our differences.

6 We pledge to address issues when they need to be addressed, in a professional way, respecting people's opinions and feelings. We bring the truth – what we really think – into the room. We never say anything behind each other's backs that we would not say to each other's faces. We see and respect others' points of view, while having the courage to share our own.

7 When we make decisions, they should be 'true decisions', i.e. we do not keep revisiting them. Everyone buys into those decisions, after they have been given a chance to voice their opinions, and supports them.

8 We know that whatever we think or say, it is what we do that really matters. When we make mistakes, we take a different action without dwelling on the past.

9 We know that unless we adhere to this agreement, our customers will not trust us and not buy from us, and our business will suffer.

10 In the event of a dispute, we will have a clear method for its resolution.

Signed _____   Date _____

Signed _____   Date _____

RESOLVING DISPUTES

Television audiences can't have enough 'real-life' programmes thrown at them. Anything with conflict goes down particularly well. We have *Car Wars*, *Neighbours at War*, and it may be only a matter of time before we have *The Office Wars*.

Not a very catchy title, perhaps, but no shortage of examples.

And with every example, a dream, ambition or lifetime's work is potentially shattered.

In any company, especially one full of ambitious entrepreneurs, the potential for conflict, disputes and negative publicity soars.

This depressing reality can be avoided, not just by neutralizing such fallouts in advance, but by being clear and in agreement as to what to do in the event of any dispute.

You have three alternatives: mediation, arbitration and separation.

1 Mediation: between yourselves or facilitated by other(s)

This will only work if and only if there are two different points of view, and those holding each point are in agreement that they want to reach a resolution. They make a commitment to each other, and the others involved in the company, that the dispute will be resolved.

The two parties in dispute meet behind closed doors, on their own or with one or more members of the company or an independent outsider.

There is one 'ground rule': no-one leaves the room until either the issue is resolved or you have exhausted the following process (in which case go to 2 Arbitration).

- Each person takes turns, stating their own point of view, and their desired result/outcome. They can talk for as long as they want, and must not be interrupted.
- If others are present to help resolve this dispute, they can ask questions after both people involved in the dispute have spoken.
- Next, each person states the point of view of the other person, as if they are the other person. This helps the person to see the other point of view, to get a feel for how the other person feels and helps them to articulate just the facts involved. (This technique was used in the process that brought peace to Northern Ireland.)
- Finally, the two people discuss, and keep discussing their points of view about the issues involved until one of two things happen – they reach an agreement, which usually has to be some form of compromise, or they do not, in which case they go forward to 2 Arbitration.

Note: If one other person or more people are present, they can help in the mediation process.

2 Arbitration

Arbitration may either follow on from mediation, or be used as a first stage if one party does not commit to reaching a resolution by mediation. It can also be useful in situations where there are more than two points of view involved.

Arbitration is where a third party or a group of people, or an agreed prearranged process, is used to reach an agreement. The third party – who may be independent of the company, or a nominated person from within it – looks at the issues, examines the facts and listens to both parties. They then make a decision that is binding on everyone involved, by discussion or by a vote.

I have seen disputes effectively resolved in this way. The people in dispute have a small audience of trusted others who form the resolution for them.

If the dispute cannot be resolved in any other way, agree to toss a coin, roll a dice or turn a playing card. This is a last resort and may not sound very satisfactory, but as long as the process is agreed upon in advance, it has a chance of working.

3 Separation

I have often likened starting a company to starting a marriage, except there may be more than two parties involved in starting a business!

Sometimes colleagues cannot resolve their differences. No amount of talking, listening and independent help can take them forward.

In this case separation may be the answer. Some people simply cannot work together, and admitting this will avoid future hassle and problems.

If this happens, agree to differ, and agree to no negative publicity and to never speak of the dispute again. This enables both parties to move forward without any baggage.

I know of scores of companies that have failed because someone leaving felt they were not treated properly and they would rather make sure that no-one achieves anything than let the remaining people succeed.

This seems especially true of entrepreneurs. Hell hath no fury like an entrepreneur scorned!

Overall, whatever you decide, always see things from one another's point of view, demonstrate appropriate business acumen throughout, and keep all issues in perspective.

The first serious business dispute I helped resolve was between the chairman and the chief executive of a large organization. I met with them each individually beforehand and established that they both 'hated' each other and were both committed to resolving the dispute! And they had to do this, fast.

So, I booked a private meeting room in a hotel and cleared the room of everything apart from two chairs and a table in the corner. I met with them in the room and told them they were to stay in this room until one of two things happened: they either resolved to work together, or one of them would resign. I would be outside the door, ensure they were fed and watered, but neither of them would be allowed to leave until they reached one of those two outcomes.

With that, I closed the door, sat guard and ... three hours and seven minutes later, they told me they had resolved their relationship. I sat with them while they committed to each other, and to me, on how they would go forward.

And before you ask yourself, the room was en suite...

YOUR THREE KEY ACTIONS

- Be nice to people you do not have to be nice to, starting today.
- Have a relationship with money that attracts it into your life, value it as energy, a symbol of success. Decide, truly decide, to be happy, to have money and to make a difference to others.
- Form trusted relationships and treat people with respect. If you fall out with a business colleague do something about it, early.

The Journey of Hindsight continues at IV Your Warning! – 12 How to Never Be Found Out (by 'reality') on page 145.

The Journey of Misadventure continues at V Your Secrets – 15 How to See What Is Hidden in Plain Sight on page 177.

YOUR BRAND – DESIGN A GLOBAL BRAND

'Everything that can be invented has been invented.'
Charles H. Duell, Commissioner, US patent office,
1899

SUMMARY
Find and pursue your big idea. When you have it you will know. This idea will become your focus, your life and to a degree your very self. It does not have to be original. Your idea will be something very special to you – start to think about the value your idea can bring to other people and organizations.

You have decided to make money, and to help others, by simply being yourself.

It is a true decision. You are really going to commit to it.

Sorry, that should have read: Is it a true decision? Are you really going to commit to it?

Read that line again. How do you feel as you do so?

You have decided to make money, and help others, by simply being yourself.

Because how you feel at this moment on your journey is absolutely critical: what you think in your head, what you say to yourself about what you are reading, and most fundamentally of all, how you feel in your heart – in yourself.

True decisions are always made on the basis of emotion – how people feel. We then stack up the logic afterwards, to back up our decision.

Your customers (and you are going to need plenty of those) make buying decisions based on how they feel – often in a moment of high emotion.

And your big idea, the one that you are going to serve, while it serves you, will most probably come to you in such a moment.

Yes, logic plays a part, as an assistant to your emotions, if you like. If you consider yourself to be logical rather than emotional, you are choosing to believe that because it makes you feel more comfortable, emotionally.

You are not as logical as you may think – if you were, you wouldn't spend so much time wondering and worrying about things that have gone wrong in the past, that you cannot change, or so much time worrying and wondering what might go wrong in the future, when you know the future has not happened yet.

Let's find your big idea, and let's find it right now, and turn it into a business that adds value to other people, while making money for you.

WHAT DRIVES YOU?

Why do you want to be an entrepreneur?

Why do you want to be a millionaire?

Why do you want to do what you want to do?

If you don't know what drives you, why you are doing something, you will find it difficult to come up with an idea that is big enough and that you are passionate about. There are four methods to help you identify this further on in this chapter.

It is not the most intelligent who succeed; it's the ones who have the drive, determination and passion. For example, everyone knows what to do to lose weight: eat less and exercise more. Success is about having the confidence and determination to do it, borne through passion and commitment.

Once you have found, decided on and committed to a specific idea, it will be yours to be passionate about ... until you find one day that it doesn't do it any more for you.

Then... revisit this chapter and get a new purpose.

Entrepreneurs often change direction because what they are doing is no longer interesting, challenging or fun. Richard Branson started with a student magazine and now runs an airline. There's no right or wrong here – only what works and what doesn't. What are your dominating thoughts and ideas? What do you spend your day telling yourself? It matters far more than you might think.

Here's how Napoleon Hill explained it:

> *'Any dominating idea, plan, or purpose held in your conscious mind through repeated effort and emotionalized by a burning desire for its realization is taken over by the subconscious and acted upon through whatever natural and logical means may be available.'*

Pull together what you think about most, what you really want and your aims in life by using one or more of the following four techniques. By doing this, you will bring together what may have previously seemed like just random thoughts, and move towards your big idea – the outcome of what you want to achieve.

1 What really drives you?

Ask yourself:

- What do I want?
- What will that do for me?
- Why is that important to me?

Keep going through these questions repeatedly – over and over – until you start to get the same or consistent answers.

Don't read on until you do this, no matter how long it takes, or how strange it may seem. Get to the point when you have a clear and consistent response coming back at you.

The following is a transcript of a conversation with a client I was working with in the Middle East, who does not wish to be named. This actual session lasted nine rounds before we got a consistent, authentic response.

Round 1
'What do you want?'

'I want to help others.'

'What will that do for you?'

' It will keep me busy.'

'Why is that important to you?'

'I like to be busy.'

(Note the mix of politically correct and almost flippant answers – this is normal in the early stages of this exercise.)

We carried on, round and round, with lots of pauses, and always a variation on the words.

Round 4
'What do you want?'

'I want to help others to learn more languages than their own.'

'What will that do for you?'

'It will help them, and me, to prove it is possible.'

'Why is that important to you?'

'Because my teacher at school always told me I was useless at languages.'

(Note this is getting much more personal, and in that last answer we have found one of his key drivers – at this point I knew we were getting closer to the real issues.)

Round 8
'What do you want?'

'I want to help others to understand the power and beauty of spoken language.'

'What will that do for you?'

'It will help further my own, and other people's understanding, and it will make me happy and make my children really proud of me.'

'Why is that important to you?'

'Because I can show everyone who has ever been told they can't learn languages, that they can, while getting paid good money, and because I love my boys.'

Now we repeat once more and this is the consistent and real answer.

2 Discover your passion with just three questions

As you answer these questions, go with your gut feeling. Do not analyse the questions or their meaning; just go with your first thoughts, your instinct.

Your instinct can serve you well. It is the sum total of every experience you have ever been through in your life, combined with every piece of knowledge you have ever learned. So it is very important, and worth listening to. But, hey, you already know that, because you remember the number of times that you had such a gut feeling, then spent hours, days or weeks of analysis, delay and logical thinking, only to return to where you were in the first place.

- What excites me?
- What do I talk about, most?
- If I knew I simply could not fail, what would I do?

Years ago when I was working for a large company, I noticed a member of my team, Clive, who was not very excited with his work. Actually, he looked bored stiff, and although he delivered some good work, it was clear he would rather be having deep root canal surgery at his dentist than do what he was doing.

I sat down with him one day at lunch and, after the usual pleasantries, we had the following exchange:

'So, Clive, what excites you?'

(Pause) 'I don't know.'

(Longer pause) 'What do you talk about, most?'

'My hobby.'

'What's that?'

'I love boats.'

He then spoke about sailing, water and every related topic until he delivered the killer line: 'I also love it because I am the treasurer of my yacht club, and my other passion is accounts – numbers and figures.'

An idea came into my mind; rather than me tell him my idea, I wanted to know his:

'If you knew you simply could not fail, what would you do?'

'I would work with accounts, but I am not qualified in any way.'

Not qualified in any way! This man, who had sat quietly in the corner of my department, delivering average quality work with never a smile, had come alive, that was qualification enough. And he had just told me he was the treasurer of a large yacht club – what more qualification did he need?

I asked him there and then. 'Would you like to help me with our annual budgets, which I absolutely hate doing and always fail to get agreement from the Finance Director on what we really need.'

He just smiled, a huge smile.

From that moment on I seemed to get more success in driving through my budgets, and Clive is now a successful consultant helping information technology directors to do the same.

3 What brings you truly 'into the moment'?

What fulfils you? What would make life perfect for you? What fills you with absolute joy and/or total peace?

It could be a state of mind, or state of being, or simply something that you love to do so much that, when you do it, your mind does not wander, you are present in the moment.

On the next page write down the first ten words or actions or experiences that come to mind.

Examples:

- Being in total control of how I spend my time.
- Meeting someone who has been written off in life.
- Helping someone with a message they might not otherwise hear.
- Being about to go and speak to 5000 people.
- Having the financial security to help others less fortunate than myself.
- Writing the very first sentence of a new book.

Now look through the list to spot a recurring theme, and/or go through the list again and prioritize in the right-hand column – just prioritize, no more guidance than that is needed.

1		
2		
3		
4		
5		
6		
7		
8		
9		
10		

4 Let life show you the way

With this method, you stop asking questions. You don't do any tests or write anything down.

You simply throw your question out there, to the universe – you choose the question, one that really means something to you, one that's been burning away. Here are some suggestions:

- What's my purpose?
- What's the big idea that I am looking for?
- What should I do with my life?

Only ask one question.

Ask it three times, in silence or out loud (perhaps best not on a crowded train).

And then – and this is key – ask it no more, just wait for an answer.

From that moment, for a period of one whole week, take very special notice of everything that happens around you: the people you meet, the things that happen, the things you notice. Pay attention to every event, person and thing, in every moment you can.

> 'We see what we expect to see, not necessarily what's really there ... makes you wonder how many other things are right in front of you – sights, sounds, smells – that you can't experience because you have been conditioned not to ... your brain's wiring is like the Interstate highway system – it's easy to go from one well-travelled place to another – but the places in between, off the highway, even though they are there, most people just zip right past them.'
> From the film *Interstate 60*, written by Bob Gale

Note: If you want to know why this works, see Journey V Your Secrets: See What Others Don't, starting on page 155.

At this stage you may be on your way to having or developing your big idea, or you may not have started yet. Where you are on your journey doesn't matter. What matters is that deep down you know you may have something that you can use to make you a Naked Millionaire, even if you haven't yet decided exactly what it is.

However, there may be other questions that you now ask yourself, as you may think of ideas.

* What if I have an idea that is not 'original?'
* What if there are lots of people already doing what I may think of?

If that is the case, do it better, do it differently, or design a unique approach to it – all as long as the core idea is not someone else's intellectual property. You would not be permitted to release a new software system and call it Windows New, just as you could not rearrange the words in *The Da Vinci Code* and call it your own.

That still leaves you plenty of scope.

Right now, you need to be convinced that what you have come up with is fine for this stage in your personal journey.

When I first wrote *The Naked Leader* I decided my big idea was 'leadership'.

That word and concept excited me after many years of boring process, procedure and management in organizations. 'Leadership', yes, that was it! So I went to Google and searched under the term 'leadership', and got:

Results 1–10 of about 94,000,000 for leadership

That figure has risen today (seven years later) to 123,000,000 results.

I had to find an original angle on a well-worn term and in a crowded marketplace, which I believe we did: 'leadership by being the best that you already are'.

Seemed common sense at the time, and still does.

If you have come up with a general subject area or a loose concept as your idea, that is fine. We can hone it down later.

Also, do not think that 'original' or 'first to market' always wins. In fact, it rarely does. Johnson and Johnson invented the first disposable nappy/diaper, and sold it to a niche market of 1% of parents with small babies. Ten years later (yes, ten years) along came Proctor and Gamble with 'Pampers' – and took 95% of the same market.

Only one person or company can be first to market with a new idea. That's not to say that many others can't follow, improving on the original and offering something new, better value, perhaps marketed more effectively, saving on development costs.

Do you think there were other record shops around before Richard Branson opened his first Virgin shop? Xerox launched the first photocopy machine and took the market by storm; Canon positioned their product for a home and small business market (no threat to Xerox then), and captured the market across the board, from home user to corporate.

The first mass-produced digital audio player (DAP) was created in 1997 by SaeHan Information Systems, which sold its 'MPMan' player in the middle of 1998. This was followed later in the same year by the Rio PMP300, made by Diamond Multimedia.

As you read this, are you enjoying your MPMan or Rio? Or are you perhaps listening to music on an iPod, launched in October 2001, a full three years later (in technology terms, a lifetime)?

MP3 stands for MPEG-1 audio layer 3, like you care, unless of course you do, because that might be your big idea, or it might be more general like 'electrics' or 'coaching' or based on a hobby, 'fishing' or...

> *'It's easy to forget that before there were famous fashion designers there were nameless manufacturers who made beautiful products.'*
> *Chasing Cool* by Noah Kerner and Gene Pressman

Tom Minter is the founder of SocksForHappyPeople.com. He says:

'The key to success for any entrepreneur is to add value. The more value an entrepreneur adds by solving people's problems and improving the quality of their lives, the more that entrepreneur will be rewarded. This is a fundamental principle and will apply for all time.'

Reproduced with permission of Tom Minter.

What value does your big idea offer? To other people, to organizations, to the world? What pain (difficulty) that people have will your idea help to reduce, or, ideally remove? What pleasure (opportunity) will your idea help to increase, or, ideally, make permanent for people?

Think on those questions as you do two other things:

- Enjoy a glass of your favourite tipple as a 'well done' for coming up with your big idea – you are already in a very small percentage of people who follow through, and you are further down your journey than others; and
- Share your idea – I know you are dying to – so go now and share it with your dog, or cat, or horse, or other animal, or a brick wall, or a mirror, or anything that will keep it secret. Only share it with a human being if you totally trust them.

Ewan McFarlane founded www.metsuki.co.uk, and revolutionized an existing idea.

I'm not an optician, am I?
My working life began managing farms and progressed to consulting for multinationals around the world, hardly your conventional career path in optics. Now looking back it's possible to see two, small, random, unconnected but nevertheless life-changing events.

En route home from Moscow via Victoria Station, I was really excited about collecting my first pair of glasses, the latest titanium hi-tech rimless design, worn by astronauts no less. What would this do for my image in the boardroom? Absolutely nothing! They didn't fit properly and the sales assistant persuaded me it was my fault because I chose them. Consigning them to a drawer, I soon forgot about the glasses but not about the experience and how it made me feel.

Years later, working for a regional enterprise agency, I was tasked to give marketing advice to a company whose business was fitting prescription lenses to spectacle frames. In the process I learned the basic economics of a dispensing optician.

One morning soon after, I woke up energized after dreaming about an online prescription glasses business with great customer service, and so it began.

Five years later, every day brings new challenges and new rewards and we grow in our business and in ourselves.

www.metsuki.co.uk

YOUR THREE KEY ACTIONS

- Find, and decide to pursue, your big idea using one of the four methods, or a combination of them. Listen to your heart – your head can catch up later.
- At this stage do not worry about whether or not it is original – think of an angle on it later.

- Think about how your idea can help other people or organizations, move away from 'pain' (what they want less of) towards 'pleasure' (what they want more of).

The Journey of Hindsight continues at VII Your Book – 19 How to Begin Writing a Book (and finish it!) on page 231.

The Journey of Misadventure continues at IV Your Speaking – 16 How to Prepare (Not for the timid!) on page 191.

HOW TO BECOME AN OBVIOUS EXPERT (IN A WORLD FULL OF THEM)

'An expert is someone who knows some of the worst mistakes that can be made in their subject, has made a few of them, and knows how to avoid them.'

Werner Karl Heisenberg

'It pays to be obvious, especially if you have a reputation for subtlety.'

Isaac Asimov

SUMMARY

You must know a lot or learn a lot about your chosen subject (your big idea). You must have experience and be able to think on the spot. People need to know about you, where to find you and what you stand for. They will then be able to talk about you, recommend and review you. Have a point of view, be clear in all you say and do, provoke interaction, and be humble. Finally, while most publicity is helpful, there is such a thing as bad publicity. If you don't want something to appear in the papers, then don't do it in the first place.

Obvious *(adj): easily seen, recognized, or understood; open to view or knowledge; evident. Antonyms: hidden.*
Expert*: a person who has special skill or knowledge in some particular field; specialist; authority. Antonyms: unskillful.*

www.dictionary.com

After looking up the above, I had to check the meaning of 'antonym' – it means opposite – because I didn't know.

I do now, but that doesn't make me an expert on words; and if I am not an 'expert' by my own definition, then I can hardly be an 'obvious expert' by someone else's.

This is your journey to becoming an 'obvious expert' – and that splits into two parts:

- *Performance* – knowing enough about your subject, to the extent that you can write about it with authority, speak about it in a way that your audience understands, and form opinions in contentious areas. People need order – they crave order – in their lives, and they are relieved when they find an expert who knows what they are talking about.
- *Perception* – you need to be recognized by other people, potential customers/clients, and in the wider world, as *'an* obvious expert', or, if you are feeling a little less humble, *'the* obvious expert'. This is about your credibility in the eyes of others. You are credible when people recommend you, when your knowledge is asked for or referred to, particularly by, your customers, your peers, or in the media.

Performance and perception – if you are to achieve your dream, you can't have one without the other.

I would love to share a story about a hidden expert, but I couldn't find one!

If you decide to become an 'expert' in your own opinion, and somehow manage to persuade others (through persuasion, propaganda and bullshit), the consequences are that sooner or later, you will be found out. Once that happens, you will never recover – so if you want another shot at it, change your name, move to another country and choose a different subject area of expertise.

This guy wasn't intending to be an 'expert', but because he was being treated as such (being asked questions) it took a little while to discover what had really happened.

THE GRADUATE 'EXPERT'

In May 2006 Guy Goma, a graduate from the Congo, arrived at the BBC for an interview to work with them in information technology.

Due to a mixup at Reception, he instead appeared on the BBC's *News 24* in place of an IT expert who had failed to turn up. At the time he assumed this was part of his interview process and so he carried on...

He was asked three questions on air about the Apple court case (Apple Software vs Apple recording label); he assumed this was part of the interview and his answers seemed sensible!

Mr Goma said his interview was 'very short', but he was prepared to return to the airwaves and was 'happy to speak about any situation'.

HOW TO BECOME AN OBVIOUS EXPERT

To be an obvious expert you have to have knowledge, experience and imagination.

Knowledge

Of course you may already have a good deal of knowledge around your 'big idea' based on experience and expertise. But can you write and talk about it with ease and with passion, and make it relevant to others? Keep learning and being open to new ideas, angles and opinions in your area of expertise.

You can never know everything that you need to know about your chosen area of excellence, but you must know quite a lot! Your knowledge needs to be grounded, not just in academia, but also in the real worlds of business, organizations and life. If you want to be an *obvious expert*, and not just an *academic expert*, knowledge alone is not enough. As an expert you must know how to apply it, and how to help others apply it.

In ancient Greece, Socrates was reputed to hold knowledge in high esteem. One day an acquaintance met the great philosopher and said, 'Do you know what I just heard about your friend?'

'Hold on a minute,' Socrates replied. 'Before telling me anything I'd like you to pass a little test. It's called the Triple Filter Test.'

'Triple filter?'

'That's right,' Socrates continued. 'Before you talk to me about my friend, it might be a good idea to take a moment and filter what you're going to say. That's why I call it the triple filter test. The first filter is Truth. Have you made absolutely sure that what you are about to tell me is true?'

'No,' the man said, 'actually I just heard about it and ...'

'All right,' said Socrates. 'So you don't really know if it's true or not. Now let's try the second filter, the filter of Goodness. Is what you are about to tell me about my friend something good?'

'No, on the contrary...'

'So,' Socrates continued, 'you want to tell me something bad about him, but you're not certain it's true. You may still pass the test though, because there's one filter left: the filter of Usefulness. Is what you want to tell me about my friend going to be useful to me?'

'No, not really...'

'Well,' concluded Socrates, 'if what you want to tell me is neither true nor good nor even useful, why tell it to me at all?'

Experience

Have you ever noticed, when it comes to a debate over whether knowledge or experience is more important, people with knowledge say knowledge, and people with experience say experience?

There's a surprise!

As an *obvious expert*, you need both.

You will be expected by customers, clients, and investors to have lots of experience – so if you haven't got any, go get some, and if you haven't got much, go get some more.

You must also have made some mistakes – if you haven't, you will never achieve the status of 'obvious' because no-one will believe you. Everyone makes mistakes. Also, these experiences are critical in order for you to have a deeper understanding of your area of expertise, and most crucially to be able to help others.

I was interviewing the final shortlist of three candidates for a global programme management company. Hidden in the middle of my questions was the most important question:

'Tell me about a really big mistake that you, personally, made.'

It is a fairly common question, and in many 'perfect answers for the perfect interview' type books the recommended answer is almost universally the same (the 'good answer' below). Here is a range of common answers, working up to one that landed the job:

The very weak answer

'I have never made any mistakes; I pride myself on getting everything right'.

This person at best takes no risks, doesn't actually do anything, or at worst, is a liar.

The weak answer

'Once, my team didn't…' or 'someone else failed to…'

This person is avoiding the question and shifting the blame onto others. The question was about a mistake that you, personally, made.

The OK answer

'On a project once, I held things up by two whole days by asking for a more detailed plan. However, in the end that was just what was needed...' (They then add more detail.)

This person focuses on a mistake they made which turned out not to be a mistake at all – probably the most common technique used by candidates. And remember, 'most common' does not stand out from the crowd.

The good answer

'Yes, I once made a mistake with some scheduling work – I had to work through the night to rectify it.'

This person has read the books! They give an example of a mistake they made, and how they subsequently turned it around.

The answer that got one person the job

'I have made many mistakes in my time; let me tell you about the biggest.' They then go on with honesty and emotion – almost like a confessional – to recount a near disaster, or indeed a disaster, how they coped, what the outcome was and the lessons they learned from it.

World-class project managers have scars on their backs. Those scars are deep, they are life-long, and they are what separate the good from the outstanding.

'People only think about me as the person who made that one terrible mistake ... it's a bit unfair because I made many more mistakes which I'm not credited for.'
Gerald Ratner

Imagination

Your imagination will play a huge part on your journey to being an obvious expert.

You may not always be able to recount the sum total of all of your knowledge or to remember a relevant experience, at a moment's notice – this is where your imagination kicks in.

When I write 'imagination' in this context, I mean a combination of interpretation, gut feel (the combination of your life's experiences and knowledge) and invention (making something up).

Note that I use the word 'combination' – as an obvious expert you will use a mix of all three, while providing an answer that is understandable by a ten-year-old.

Here's an example. You are an obvious expert in business leadership, and you are on a panel discussion.

Question: 'What are the three biggest challenges being faced by finance leaders at the moment?'

The chairman says your name. The first thing you do is 'interpret' the question logically – the question has asked for the *three biggest challenges faced by finance leaders today, right now.*

(A common pitfall is to re-interpret for the question to suit the answer you want to give, or have thought up. I have done this myself. Question: 'David, what is the single most important action to take...?' Me (not being an obvious expert, rather being a smart ass): 'I will give you the most common.'

No! The person asked for the most important, not common. I did not answer their question, and made it worse by being presumptuous, insulting and big-headed.)

Back to the question you are being asked – two challenges come to mind – profitability and saving costs, both key in all economic times. However, these only total two challenges and you need *three*!

This is where your imagination kicks in:

You are an *obvious expert*, so what do you think (imagine) the third one might be? Of course you can't make up complete nonsense, because what you say will be treated as near gospel (you are an obvious expert, after all); also, those first two thoughts are a very dry response.

And so you might respond:

'Profitability and cost savings are important in all economic climates, and it is always a challenge to know what is keeping the CEO awake at night, without actually needing to be there!'

EXPERTS

The word 'expert' is used freely these days, which makes it hard to tell who the real experts are. Here's a checklist used by Alan Stevens when he's looking for real experts:

- Experience – I look for someone who has been working in an area for many years. You can't become an expert overnight (except maybe on Twitter, which has only been around for a short time).
- Eloquence – I like experts who can articulate their ideas in a language I can understand.
- Evidence – Articles, books, TV appearances and a body of work all point to the fact that a person is an 'acknowledged expert'.
- Endorsement – Testimonials from real people in real companies, saying what the expert did for them.
- Empathy – An ability to understand people's problems, and a willingness to help.

Adapted from Alan Stevens – President-Elect, Global Speakers Federation, author of *Ping!* and *The Pocket Media Coach*.
www.alanstevens.net

FOUR FACTORS SHARED BY ALL OBVIOUS EXPERTS

1 Humility

As an *obvious* expert you do not have to oversell yourself. You do not need to shout out to the world about how good you are; you do not have to boast *at all*.

This can prove to be a fine balance to achieve – combining humility with being the expert in the room. Share what you know, help people with what you know and what you have experienced, without saying how 'right' you were, or how 'good' you are.

A senior manager in a large retail company invited me in to speak about a 'very confidential' issue. He asked me if I could help with staff morale in his flagship store.

I was just starting out in what I do, and I was very flattered to be asked. However, I was also worried that after I left he might change his mind – I had to make sure he was convinced I could do this. And so I blurted out 'Easy!'

He looked at me and said 'Easy? If it was "easy" we would have done it ourselves.'

I lost the sale for appearing to be so big-headed and flippant.

When I have been asked to do something similar since, I just say 'thank you' and then move on to discuss the detail.

As an *obvious expert*, you do not have to boast about your experience, your qualifications or the size of your brain. If you do the latter, people will assume it to be very small!

Yes, you will have to market yourself, and when you do, let your experience, clients and achievements speak for themselves.

And when you are invited into the room, you are there because you are an *obvious expert* – that's enough. Indeed, the very best experts will make sure that other people in the room shine, that ideas are other people's, not their own.

2 Having a point of view

As an obvious expert it is *your* point of view that people want to hear – as I discovered for myself on a day I will remember forever, no matter how hard I want to forget it.

It was my first major workshop after writing the book. The event company had not downplayed my expertise – 'The IT Director's Masterclass' was the billing and the marketing had gone well; we had over 30 IT directors attend. Gulp! That's over 30 senior executive decision-makers who really knew their subject, in a room with me, for two whole days, because I had written a book.

OK, I also had 20 years in IT behind me as well, but that was a few years before, and in information technology, that is a lifetime!

I prepared for this one like never before. I rehearsed, and when the first day arrived, I was ready. It started well, I set the scene, made a few self-deprecating jokes, and got them on my side.

The opening went well, and it took a whole hour before I was asked by a delegate:

'David, what's your view on the difference between leadership and management?'

The room waited, expectantly, people even lifted their pens, ready for my view.

I bottled it.

'Well, I began, Jack Welch said…' I then went into Jack's thoughts on the subject, then Richard Branson and finally Donald Trump. Phew, I thought, I am glad I had read up on them before the day.

And it was now time for the first break; I had 'got out of jail free'!

John Blake, now my friend of many years, was running the event under the banner of his company MTS Ltd. John gives very frank feedback.

He was now walking towards me, face like thunder.

DT: 'Hi John, I think that went OK.'

JB: 'Well, I don't, and neither do they.'

(Pause)

DT: 'They seem happy enough.'

JB: 'Happy enough...' (pause) 'Happy enough? Is that what we put in the brochure – is that what we promised them, David? Invest your hard-earned money by spending time with David Taylor, the obvious expert in leadership and IT, and we promise that you will be happy enough.'

DT: 'OK, help me. What should I do?'

JB: 'I will tell you exactly what to do. These people have paid to see you, to hear from you, to be with you – if they wanted to know what Richard Branson thinks about this or that, they would have gone to see Richard Branson. They haven't, they have come to see you – so, from now on, you tell them what you think, why and how they can apply what you think in their day-to-day work. Got that?'

Possibly the best single piece of advice I ever received in my life.

As an *obvious expert*, you are not a facilitator (although you will facilitate), you are not a trainer (although you will impart knowledge) – you are a specialist, a unique expert in a specific field of expertise.

In these days of knowledge saturation, many people want you to just get to the point, tell them what to do and offer clear practical actions they can make real as soon as possible.

Got that?

3 Being brief

Obvious experts get to the point, give clear and often brief responses. It's enough to be understood, no more.

Get to the point, and get to the point really fast. Never use ten words where five will do. Never use jargon (a word that someone hearing it would not understand), speak as if you are speaking to a ten-year-old, and ten-year-olds know a great deal.

News channels can describe a war in a headline, so you and I can describe anything in the same time.

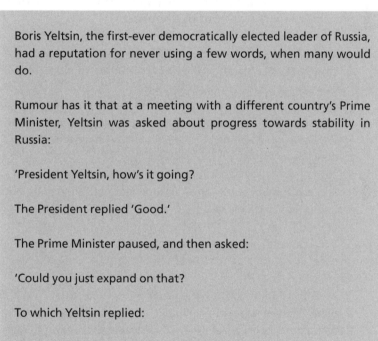

Boris Yeltsin, the first-ever democratically elected leader of Russia, had a reputation for never using a few words, when many would do.

Rumour has it that at a meeting with a different country's Prime Minister, Yeltsin was asked about progress towards stability in Russia:

'President Yeltsin, how's it going?

The President replied 'Good.'

The Prime Minister paused, and then asked:

'Could you just expand on that?

To which Yeltsin replied:

'Not good.'

4 Facilitating interaction

While people will want to hear your thoughts, your expertise will increase in the eyes of others when you encourage people to interact and offer their views.

People enjoy sharing with each other, having lively debate and discussion. The more you facilitate this, without intervening with an 'answer', the bigger the difference you make and the higher your credibility becomes.

As a facilitator, you are required to know all the possible answers while allowing the others to play their game, intervening only when asked to. Be clear what your audience, your delegates, your customers want out of the process.

I was booked to 'speak' at the House of Commons in the UK, inside a private room, with around 20 MPs from across all different parties. I started by sharing my belief that 'no matter what your age, your experience or your background, everything you need, to achieve anything you want in your life, you already have within you, right now.'

This is a statement designed to provoke reaction, debate and action. And it certainly did!

They were off – discussion, debate, disagreement – with one another. It was if I was not there.

After five minutes of this (the session was scheduled for just half an hour) I started to worry – nay, panic – this was getting out of control, going horribly off script. How would I cover everything I needed to cover? Am I earning my money by making one statement and then just allowing them to fill the time by themselves?

True, I interjected, I offered my opinion, I made sure I facilitated some of the quieter people to make sure they had a say. I got across many of my supporting evidence and messages, in the form of a conversation.

And then, suddenly, there was a knock at the door. The Master at Arms did not wait for a response, he was in the room and saying 'Ladies and gentlemen, your time is up, we have to lock up now'. Immediate silence.

That's it, I decided, what a screw-up.

Then they turned to me, as one, and said 'Thank you', 'What a wonderful evening', 'We have learned a lot tonight'.

MAKING IT HAPPEN FOR YOU

Becoming an obvious expert can take time – time to build a reputation, get good feedback and recommendation, and to be asked back again. Here are some ways you can build your platform and start letting the world know who you are and what you've got to say:

- Write a letter to your local paper, or a national paper, on your subject, and offer a point of view. You may be surprised at how few letters local papers receive; they will be keen to print something interesting, controversial or topical.
- Contribute to a blog (short for weblog) that is active in your area of interest and expertise. Or even better, start your own and drive the agenda in your field. Remember to maintain it once you've started – it's not good for potential clients to find the latest online contributions you've made are over two years old.
- If you want a printed column in a newspaper, magazine, corporate newsletter or academic journal, then write a letter to the editor (not an email) and ask for one. Describe what's in it for the readers and why you are the person to write it. Expect and welcome rejections. Write a first column example and send it in. Be persistent, and, on your road to becoming an obvious expert, don't always expect to get paid. Retain editorial control and have joint copyright with the magazine or paper. If you can't negotiate a fee, negotiate something else – advertising space for your next event, or free copies for your clients. If you don't ask, you won't get.
- Get on Twitter (see Chapter 6 page 71).

- Get on the radio. Call a radio phone-in programme. When you get through you will first speak with a researcher who will ask what point you want to make – angle your comment as different from what has been broadcast so far, to maximize your chances of being put on air. When you are speaking, do so as if you are talking one to one with a friend.
- Get on TV. With the immediacy and volume of news, channels are keen to hear from 'experts' in a particular area. Wait for a news story that relates to your topic and fax all of the news channels with a ten-line (maximum) biography describing yourself. When you are on, tell them the words that will appear in caption below your name – something like '(your name), adviser and expert on (subject)' – in this instance it will look as if the channel are referring to you as an expert, not yourself.
- On both radio and TV, be prepared, be provocative, and have a sound-bite – the media love sound-bites – with facts to back up what you say. Never, ever swear, avoid jokes (tell stories instead) and be clear, concise and compelling. Work on your voice. Vary it, speak with passion. Remember that listeners and viewers will have one main question: 'Why should I care?' Answer that question and you will be remembered.
- 'There is no such thing as bad publicity.' Never have eight words told such a lie. This is going to sound very direct, so sorry about that. Here you are, working very hard to become an obvious expert – don't screw it up in a single moment. Your reputation that may have taken years to establish can turn to dust in a single moment.So my direct advice is this: If you don't want to see yourself on the front page (or indeed, any page) of a tabloid newspaper involved in a scandal, or similar, then *don't do it* in the first place.
- Take up positions of responsibility and influence. It could be social, as a director, or in a top position within a club or hobby that is important to your community; academic, as an honorary position at a school or university; or within a charity – raise money for them and publicize what they do.
- Dress as an obvious expert. Have presence. Choose your clothes carefully; you don't want to be running a seminar

dressed like a gardener – and remember this is certainly a matter of opinion, so err on the side of caution. Be well groomed and remember your hairbrush!

The flagship of the fleet had failed – its engine just stopped working one day.

The ship's owners tried one expert after another, but none of them could figure out how to fix the engine. Then they brought in an old man who had been fixing ships since he was a youngster.

He carried a large bag of tools with him, and when he arrived, he immediately went to work. He inspected the engine very carefully, top to bottom. Two of the ship's owners were there, watching this man, hoping he would know what to do.

After looking things over, the old man reached into his bag and pulled out a small hammer. He gently tapped something. Instantly, the engine lurched into life. He carefully put his hammer away. The engine was fixed!

A week later, the owners received a bill from the old man for $10,000. 'What?!' the owners exclaimed. 'He hardly did anything!' So they wrote the old man a note saying, 'Please send us an itemized bill.' The man sent a bill: 'Tapping with a hammer... $2; Knowing where to tap... $9,998.'

YOUR THREE KEY ACTIONS

- Know your chosen subject (your big idea) and have or get as much experience in it as possible.
- Have a point of view that is provocative, while being clear.
- Be humble and self-deprecating.

The Journey of Hindsight continues at III Your Business – 7 How to Do the Essentials (and not be a busy fool) on page 85.

The Journey of Misadventure continues at 6 How to Master Cyberspace (like a ten-year-old) on page 71.

HOW TO MASTER CYBERSPACE (LIKE A TEN-YEAR-OLD)

'It has become appallingly obvious that our technology has exceeded our humanity.'

Albert Einstein

SUMMARY

Use technology to communicate, interact and build up both supporters and detractors. Show your true personality online – get a website that reflects your brand values. Get on YouTube, Facebook, MySpace and Twitter; be everywhere; access to your audience is all around you in cyberspace.

Remember, you are a facilitator around an idea for your supporters; you are not a celebrity for them to fawn over. Your aim is to be a focal point, to attract groups of people who support or disagree with your ideas, and share an interest in your area of expertise.

Einstein may have been right many years ago: technology was indeed overtaking what we could do with it; indeed, it was overtaking what we imagined we could do with it.

Not any more.

Today, there is a huge dual trend happening simultaneously in the world: the search for humanity, for identity and meaning, alongside an ever-increasing demand for the latest technology.

The meeting point for these apparently divergent interests represents a massive opportunity for you.

I am not going into information technology in great detail here – that is well covered elsewhere by other people who know a lot more about it than I do. All I know, for certain, is that there is a train leaving the station and you need to be on it.

Use technology to communicate, to share, to interact, and in turn, use all of that to establish your global brand. The action for you is to get on board, now, or be left behind.

> *'Please know this, everyone: no-one will ever buy financial services over the phone.'*
> Senior manager at an international financial services company, three months before the launch of Direct Line Insurance

You *do not* need to understand what technology does, or how it works; you only need to understand what technology can do for you. The only exception to this is if your own big idea relates to technology, of course!

DID YOU KNOW?

- China will soon become the number one English-speaking country in the world.

- India has more Honours kids than America has kids.

- The top ten in-demand jobs in 2010 did not exist in 2004.

- We are currently preparing students for jobs that don't yet exist, where they will be using technologies that haven't yet been invented, in order to solve problems that we don't even know are problems yet.

- The US Department of Labor estimates that today's learner will have 10–14 jobs by the age of 38.

- 1 out of 8 couples married in the USA in 2008 met online.

- In 2009 there were 31 billion searches on Google every month (in 2006 this figure was 2.7 billion).

- The first commercial text message was sent in December 1992. Today the number of text messages sent and received every day exceeds the total population of the planet.

- The number of years it took to reach a market audience of 50 million (radio 38 years, TV 13 years, internet 4 years, iPod 3 years, Facebook 2 years).

- The number of internet devices in 1984 was 1,000... in 1992 it was 1,000,000... in 2008 it was 1,000,000,000.

- It is estimated that a week's worth of the *New York Times* contains more information than a person was likely to come across in a lifetime in the 18th century.

- The amount of new technical information is doubling every 2 years ... NTT Japan has successfully tested a fibre-optic cable that pushes the equivalent of 2660 CDs or 210 million phone calls every second.

Research by Karl Fisch, Scott McLeod, and Jeff Brenman

WHAT ARE SOCIAL MEDIA AND WHY ARE THEY IMPORTANT TO YOU?

In a nutshell, social media is people having conversations online. And these days, there are a lot of conversations going on.

In 2008 social media overtook porn as the number one activity on the web (source: www.alexa.com).

To give you some sort of idea of just how big that is, if Facebook were a country it would be the 4th most populated in the world behind China, India and the United States, having 300 million residents who log on for 6 billion minutes every day and share 2 billion pieces of content every week.

At the time of writing, on YouTube, the video-sharing social network owned by Google, 100 million videos are watched every day, and 20 hours of new content are uploaded every minute.

That's a lot of sharing, even before we've mentioned Twitter, MySpace, LinkedIn, Bebo, Tagged, Friendster, Flickr, Hi5, FriendFeed and the other 650+ social networks.

Already two-thirds of the global internet population have visited a social network, and with social media activity growing at three times the rate of internet use it is clear that, not only are social media here to stay, they represent a fundamental shift in the way the human race communicates.

'In 2008, if you're not on a social networking site, you're not on the internet.'
IAB Platform Status Report: User Generated Content, Social Media, and Advertising – An Overview, April 2008

With over 200 million blogs in cyberspace, 34% of which regularly talk about products and brands, you can be pretty sure that at some point someone will be talking about you and your company.

What will they be saying?

Will you like what you see, or will you even know what they're saying?

If you care about building your business and your global brand, you must be involved … because social media are 'word of mouth' on steroids.

WHAT'S IN IT FOR YOU?

To be honest with you, all this talk of social media does my head in. It makes me want to go and curl up in a small ball with my curly-wurly while I play with my Amstrad ZX 84.

OK, not really.

Social media are here, and more are on their way.

Go with the flow and use that 'flow' to your advantage – the internet represents a major opportunity in the way you are going to communicate with the world.

Do you find it all a bit overwhelming, all a bit too much?

Remember – as always, there is only what helps you and what does not, what pulls you closer to your goal and what pushes you further away from it. So get all this 'stuff' (a collective noun for everything I don't fully understand) to work with you and for you. The way to do that is to keep focusing on the real value that you can add, to whom, and how much that value is worth.

It's not so much that the rules have changed, or have been transformed; it's more like there are no rules anymore.

Gone forever are the days and ways of the *old media* – one-way, controlled brand messages broadcast to a mass audience. We now have *new media* – listen, participate, engage and relinquish control.

Get on board and get involved.

And when you do:

Entertain – So that people enjoy what you say, and look forward to hearing about what you do.
Educate – People like to learn something new.
Engage – Hold people's attention.
Enrich – Improve people's lives.

And, as you do, be as authentic as you would be in any interaction. Because in this new wider world, people care about who you are and what you do far more than what you say. Your aim is to be yourself, to be honest and transparent, and build a reputation around these three values. And word of reputation spreads:

'Only 14% of people trust ads, while 90% trust peer recommendations.'
Tim Lefroy, chief executive of the Advertising Association and The Nielsen Company

Be visible. Visibility builds trust, so be out there. Your customers and potential customers are on Facebook, Twitter, MySpace and others. Go and meet them there.

As an entrepreneur, as a company, you have more power at your fingertips, in real time, than you ever had before. The traditional customer/supplier relationship was face to face and the customer usually had to go to where the supplier was. Now this same relationship online means that often the supplier has to go wherever the customer is.

Public relations has also changed. The focus is now on providing fantastic customer service so that your customers go out and do your PR for you – recommend you, rate you and talk about you. Transparency and authenticity are now the key factors; ever more consumers are demanding and expecting this. And your competitors will be doing this.

'Only 14% of people trust ads, while 90% trust peer recommendations.'
Tim Lefroy, chief executive of the Advertising Association and The Nielsen Company

The power base now lies well and truly with your customers, who have more choice than ever and will change brands at the click of a mouse (Duke University research).

How do you make it happen? Cut through the jargon and hype, and do the following.

GET A WEBSITE

There are two areas you need to focus on: 'traffic' and 'conversion', two sides of the same coin.

- *Traffic* – The number of people who visit your site, who read what you say, who know about you online and think you are worth a visit. Your aim is to increase the volume of traffic to your site as much as you can, by linking to other sites and ensuring you rank highly on search engine sites (see below).
- *Conversion* – The numbers of people who make a commitment to follow you (e.g. on Twitter), to join your network, contribute to your blog, or to buy from you. Conversion involves gathering data about the people who visit your site, getting them to sign up for things and knowing something about them.

Give people a reason to visit your site, and when they are there, make sure they feel comfortable. Ensure they can get around the site with ease and without having to think too much, and above all else, involve your visitors by making your site interactive.

Ask yourself these questions:

- Is the key reason people might want to visit your website right up there, clearly emblazoned on the front page?
- Does it look like a place you would want to visit – what is the feel of the site? What you feel, your visitors will feel. Avoid using jargon, make the text a size that most people can easily read, and keep each page uncluttered.
- Is it easy to get around and navigate without thinking too much? You might want to include a 'guided tour' of the site from the homepage. Have a search facility that is not too literal.
- Is it interactive? Is there a forum for visitors to contribute to? Is there a mechanism in place for capturing information about your visitors (who they are, where they visit most often and what they are looking for)?

Drive visitors to the site

Drive visitors (traffic) to your site via SEO (search engine optimization).

I am going to share with you the three 'top secrets' of securing a prominent rank on search engines. OK, they are not secret at all; I found them by trawling the net, reading books, speaking with online entrepreneurs and with the obvious expert in this area, Lisa Forster of www.angelfysh.com.

I asked Lisa for her number-one piece of advice and this is it. *'Make sure you think about SEO before your site is built. When you are designing it, include what you need to do to ensure your site is visible to the world on every search engine.'*

HIGH PAGE RANKING

To achieve a high page ranking on search engines like Google and Bing:

1 Get lots of sites linking to your site, that are popular in themselves and cover similar areas to your site – alexa.com ranks all sites on the net by popularity. Do this by identifying a dozen sites that you think would be of interest to your visitors. Write to these sites asking for a reciprocal link (you link to them, they link to you).
2 Decide on a few key phrases (not words) and ensure that those phrases are placed early on in your text – ideally within the first 20 words, and again in the last 20 words. The key phrases will be part of your 'killer proposition', which will ideally be at the foot of every page.
3 Create viral word of mouth by having a controversial and provocative point of view around your big idea, blogging, tweeting on it and being totally transparent – i.e. what you see is what you get.

Make money through your website

Make money through your website by:

- Attracting affiliates – you sell others' products, they sell yours
- Selling advertising on your site

- Selling ebooks on your site
- Selling your products and services
- Creating a members' area or club which people pay for

GET ON TWITTER

Get on Twitter (www.twitter.com) right now.

Twitter is a form of short blogging, where people can update the world on their actions, thoughts and opinions in single 'tweets' of up to just 140 characters.

More importantly for you, Twitter is a web, social and business phenomenon, in terms of its popularity.

Tweet about your subject often. Find out who the existing 'obvious experts' are on the site and who is following them – then follow them all. Some will follow you back. Don't get insecure about having fewer followers than those you are following; it's about quality, not quantity.

Tweet on popular topics (they are listed on the sign-on page and also as 'trending topics' on the lower right-hand side once you have signed in).

GET ON FACEBOOK

Get on Facebook, MySpace or a business networking site. These are social networking websites that help you to connect friends, family and business associates. Facebook is the largest of these sites and there may be others that are more suited to your profile.

While Twitter takes time (although you can tweet when you are on the train, watching TV and maybe even on the loo), Facebook, MySpace, LinkedIn and others require a presence. They need to articulate who you are and what you stand for. They are your 'calling card' when inviting people you know and respect to join you.

On such sites, people can form groups of friends, join and form groups around a common interest, campaign or hobby. In other words, they can connect with other people around the world.

My top three tips for Facebook (these can be applied across social networking sites, including business sites) are:

- Update your status on a regular basis. Use the 'what's on your mind' page as you would share your thoughts on Twitter, and keep them brief. By doing this you join conversations, and publish interesting and relevant content.
- Protect yourself. Set your privacy settings. You can make your entire profile public for all to see, which will certainly make you visible; however, keep the following information private: photos and videos that you would not want to be seen or copied all over the web, personal financial information, details of social or family events like holidays or parties.
- Search out people on Facebook who have achieved what you want to achieve, and get tips on what they have done in terms of their profile, settings, the groups they join, and how they communicate.

For a list of business social networks visit www.nakedleader. com. One of the most widely used is www.linkedin.com. When you join such a site, be totally honest – for example, if you exaggerate your job title, someone who knows you may spot this.

Facebook campaigns are proving the power and influence of people when they group together and champion an idea. In December 2010, in the UK, husband and wife Jon and Tracy Morter started a Facebook group that would get the band Rage Against the Machine's single, 'Killing in the Name' to be the Christmas number one single, ahead of the winner of the TV reality show, *The X Factor* – despite the winner of the show having been number one in the previous four years.

USE YOUTUBE

YouTube is a video-sharing website on which users can upload and share videos.

Top video-sharing tips

- Be an authority – The more people see that you can offer free, useful and practical information, the more people will turn to you for information or advice. Submit regular videos; ensure you also put links into them from your website and in any blogs you write, plus of course on Twitter.
- Be viral – Two words that are far easier written than done! Viral videos are not usually planned. The simple rule is this: make your video different, interesting and engaging to watch, and one of them will take off. You do not need millions of viewers; a few thousand will put you in the most-watched categories.
- Explore other possibilities that YouTube offers. The great thing about these is that for every opportunity (e.g. managing your content, or starting your own channel), you will be able to watch a tutorial on how to do it.
- Comments – Under each video on YouTube, visitors have the option of leaving comments on that video. Some people seem to enjoy leaving nasty comments under videos. Remember, these are not personal; the sad people making such comments are unlikely to know you, so don't take them personally.

YOUR OVERALL AIM IS TO BUILD TRUST

Your activities start with low emotional commitment, building trust, and gradually increase until you connect with people who will pay for your advice, guidance, services and/or products.

You are now in a position to build a global organization within a matter of weeks, for very little investment, just bags of commitment, expertise and personality.

Well, why are you still reading?

YOUR THREE KEY ACTIONS

- Get on the train – almost everyone has access online, and you will realize you know more about this stuff than you may think.
- Combine technology with your big idea.
- Get a website, get on Twitter, YouTube, Facebook and MySpace.

The Journey of Hindsight continues at VI Your Speaking – 17 How to Move from Good to Great to Outstanding on page 207.

The Journey of Misadventure continues at III Your Business – 9 How to Know What to Sell (Sell it, deliver it and get paid) on page 116.

YOUR BUSINESS – START AND GROW YOUR BUSINESS

'The mechanics of running a business are really not very complicated when you get down to essentials. You have to make some stuff and sell it to somebody for more than it cost you. That's about all there is to it, except for a few million details.'

John L. McCaffrey

SUMMARY

This chapter contains everything you need to know to start a business. Read it from start to finish. No stories, no quips, no asides, just pure, full-on facts that you need to know. Starting and running and growing a business is a serious matter, and this is a very serious chapter.

Starting up even the smallest business can be unnerving. More and more of us are taking that leap – right now. Perhaps you have had been made redundant and have the drive and determination needed to make it on your own. What better or more powerful way can you prove to yourself that you are employable than by making your own business work?

Take comfort in the fact that you are not alone. Of the 4 million businesses currently in operation in the UK, more than 99% are categorized as small, with fewer than 50 employees.

To prevent this section being too long, it is written from a UK perspective. Many of the points here may differ in your country. All of the areas covered, however, need to be considered whatever country you start your business in. Your priority is to ensure you know the laws relating to business startups. Your main source of professional advice on setting up a business, on company law and finances is your accountant – more about him/her later.

TRADE AS WHAT?

First, though, what is the structure from which you want to operate?

You can be a sole trader, a limited company, a partnership or a limited liability partnership.

As a *sole trader* you are essentially self-employed. Working for yourself has benefits and of course pitfalls. Your business income will be counted alongside any existing personal income you may have, which makes accounting far more straightforward. Many people like to start out this way, as having too complex an accounting system, on top of the myriad other issues you need to deal with at startup, can be worrying enough. Let an accountant take the strain. And remember – don't get behind on your accounting!

Should you wish to make changes in the future as a sole trader, there will be less administration, less paperwork, and less stress! Of course, the big downside is that any financial problems encountered are yours to sort out alone. People you owe money to can claim personal assets such as your house. Believing in yourself and your product is key here.

In a *limited company* you are protected, to a degree, in that your own personal money is treated as separate from your company's finances. I can hear you breathing a sigh of relief there! If things go wrong, you will lose only the money you have put into the business – no-one can claim against your personal assets. In the event that you need to borrow money for expansion, though, a bank could ask you to be a guarantor as a director. You are effectively an employee of the company, with money drawn as salary or by taking profits out (known as dividends). The risk is less under the limited company umbrella, especially if you need to fund major purchases up front, so in that respect it is quite an attractive way to progress.

A *partnership* is exactly what it says on the tin: going into business with one, two or more other individuals. A partnership has fewer legal rules than a limited company, and it is less complex to set up. However, you need to have clarity in a partnership. At the start you may be very good friends and have shared enthusiasm about the road ahead; however, things can go wrong. Think of the partnership like a marriage. Draw up a partnership agreement, witnessed by a solicitor who will be able to advise on its contents. The three most important agreements are each person's roles and titles, who is putting in what to the partnership in terms of money, time and commitment, and, most of all, what happens if something goes wrong in the relationship. For example, if you are not having equal liability for debts in the partnership, you can draw up what's called a limited liability partnership.

You may think you know which routes to take; however, speak to a business adviser or an accountant. They can talk you through the options depending on the variables involved, not least the nature of your business and projected turnover.

CHOOSING A NAME

Sounds simple, doesn't it? It can be a minefield though. Your name needs to be catchy, memorable and an expression of you and what you do. You are already unique as a person. Now make the stamp on your business the same.

Forward planning is essential. Cover any future expansion eventualities. If you were to introduce new products and the name doesn't cover them, you will kick yourself and may feel obliged to change the very thing that helped you become established.

Our own trademark 'Naked Leader' actually causes us problems on the information highway because of the word 'naked'; spam filters are the bane of our life!

There are restrictions to think about too, particularly for names of limited companies. No name must be similar to one already in existence and it has to include the word limited after it. It must also pass a suitability test. For instance, you might sell Wellingtons, but Boots will be be a name you're not allowed!

You can log onto Companies House (www.companieshouse. gov.uk) to find out more about your particular sector.

Think about registering your name as a trademark in order to protect it further from reproduction. You may also consider entering your proposed name into a language translation site, to check that it doesn't mean something offensive or inappropriate in another language.

ACCOUNTING

Remember the Abba hit, 'Money, Money, Money'? Well, when you start up on your own, money will be tight. Too tight to mention even, as Simply Red once said. You need to make the money you have got, *last*. Use it as effectively as possible.

If there is one professional you would do well to part with your hard-earned cash for, it is … you've guessed it already … an accountant. A good one will pay for themselves by advising you on all the ways you can save money via tax codes, tax liabilities and other monetary considerations. This is a specialist subject; let the expert deal with it.

Make sure the accountant is reputable, likeable, someone you can get along with. Can you imagine keeping in regular touch with someone who you don't trust, or who you can't share a joke with, for instance? Ask for references from clients and detailed quotes for the various services the accountant is to provide. He/she will be vital to the success of your business, so make sure you are in constant contact. A phone call once a year at year-end is not the sort of relationship you want with someone who will be your right hand when it comes to finance.

FINDING THE RIGHT BANK

Shop around. Look at which bank offers the best services and rates for your business. You may have a long-standing relationship with one in particular, where you might have held a personal account. The better the bank knows you, the more they can help.

The devil really is in the detail. If you need to borrow money for your business, those firms that demonstrate with a robust business plan that they are able to repay a loan are more likely to be considered, with a number of other factors coming into play.

Building a relationship with your lenders and your bank is important, while getting the backing of a trusted adviser as an advocate is key. Banks look at the record of the people behind the business too, how they have managed finance in the past, and the success or otherwise of previous businesses. Showing you know your market and are aware of the competition also helps, as well as knowing the risks.

The banks will lend to strong businesses whatever the general economic market conditions. They may have become a little more selective since the financial meltdown of 2008/09, but they still lend to robust businesses. Lenders must see credible forecasts and projections, as well as evidence that you have tried to raise money yourself, through private equity or grants. This will show lenders that you are not wholly reliant on them. Spreading the risk can work in your favour too. Understanding the key criteria set by those pulling the purse strings will help you to stay one step ahead.

INSURANCE

A business adviser can help again here. Some policies are legally required while others are optional, more for peace of mind. Cost, of course, has to be a consideration. Make sure you can afford the premiums. It's also important to let your insurance company know of any changes in your circumstances, to avoid being out of pocket in the event of a claim.

Typical insurances needed by businesses are the following.

Public liability is protection from third party claims caused by injury or death, or damage done to property as a direct result of your business activities. You need to check out whether this is something you are obliged to take on board. If people are coming to your business premises, for example, this insurance is a must.

Bytestart is a portal for small business and has some useful information on public liability insurance; go to www.bytestart. co.uk/content/20/20_3/public-liability-insurance.shtml.

Employers' liability only applies if you employ someone and it covers claims arising from accidents or sickness, either on or off site. It applies only to employees. You do not have to take out this insurance if you are the sole employee of your limited company and own at least 50% of the share capital. Sole traders are also exempt, as are those who employ only close family members. Read the detail if you use temporary or seasonal workers, as they require cover.

As a general rule, an employee is someone for whom you deduct National Insurance contributions and income tax from their salary, and whose working day you control. Don't incur the wrath of the Health & Safety Executive. They will fine you if you need this insurance and you have overlooked it.

Professional indemnity is really for businesses that deliver a service, such as accountancy or legal representation, or a business acting in a professional capacity. It is designed to protect your business from legal action instigated by unhappy clients over issues such as negligence, infringement of any legal requirements or dishonesty.

Equipment insurance covers damage to equipment – for example, if someone spilt coffee over some expensive computer equipment and you had to spend thousands replacing it. If you don't like the sound of that, it's worth considering equipment insurance.

Contents insurance is standard to protect the fixtures and fittings of your premises. If you work from home, ensure your home contents policy will cover your business venture. Motor insurance is, of course, a legal requirement for all vehicles and if you use your vehicle for business you will need to state this.

Legal expenses insurance can be taken to provide protection from legal action taken against your business; this will cover you for court costs and legal fees.

As well as the few I have mentioned, there are other insurances you may wish to consider – just search online.

TAXATION

Whether you like it or not, you have to pay tax.

Limited companies are liable for Corporation Tax. It's calculated on your profits, and determined at the end of your company's financial year. You must then pay it to the Inland Revenue within nine months. Currently, the small companies' tax rate in the UK is 21% of profits (2008/09 tax year).

In the UK, Value Added Tax (VAT) is the tax added to most goods and services, and is collected at every stage of production and distribution. There will be similar taxes in most countries and you will need to check the local laws, rates and methods of collection with your accountant.

If you are a limited company director, or have employees, you will also need to be aware of the Pay as You Earn (PAYE) scheme.

It ensures that tax is deducted from your employees' pay each week or month rather than via self-assessment (which applies to sole traders). Consider National Insurance contributions too.

Self-assessment taxation is another legal requirement in what can seem like a minefield. You have to register with Her Majesty's Revenue & Customs (HMRC) when you start working for yourself. Tax is paid on the total income you receive each year.

Fill in a tax return yourself or let your accountant do it, and keep financial records to make the task of filling in the return less onerous. Things like business income records, expenses and bank and building society statements are all needed.

If you are just self-employed you will need to work out your revenue (turnover/sales) for the year and your expenses, and then calculate the tax that is due on this. Again, your accountant will know best!

I'LL RAISE YOU! HOW TO GET FINANCE

There are many ways you can raise finance for your business; explore all the options before you decide what's best for your venture.

First, ascertain what your assets and liabilities are. Know how much you need to fund your startup by forecasting your income (turnover) and expenditure on a month-by-month basis. What will be coming in and going out? The difference between what comes in and what goes out is your profit.

When you are drawing up these figures, take into account late payers, seasonal effects on sales (e.g. do you sell more in summer/hot weather, is Christmas your peak sales period of the year?) and any other factors that may affect your company. The ground rule is consider everything, dismiss nothing, and always underestimate what you will bring in and overestimate what will go out.

The choices are then various: use your savings, apply for a bank loan, consider possible government grants. You may want to start out with a low-risk strategy, working in your business part-time, while topping up your income with a regular job.

Take care when considering borrowing money; remember that remortgaging your house as security could mean your home is under threat if the very worst happens.

Overdrafts and credit cards may be expensive, and loans from family and friends should only be considered as a last resort. If you are confident that your request won't jeopardize family relationships, ensure you agree concrete terms before the loan is given.

Factoring, paying a company to give you money owed to you immediately against invoices, is another option. You pay them to pay you money that someone else owes you.

SHOW ME THE MONEY

Businesses fail because they have poor or non-existent cash flow.

Once you start experiencing cash flow problems, you can quickly fall into a rapid decline. You can't buy the raw materials, purchase the equipment you need or pay staff. Avoid being reliant on a single customer, or a very small customer base, and pay your bills on time to buy goodwill from suppliers.

There is a government ruling that means you can charge interest for late payment of monies owed to you. Make sure you state your payment terms at the bottom of every invoice, contract and order confirmation. State clear payment terms (normally 30 days, although this could be shorter or longer). Don't be shy in chasing payment and establish a positive relationship with a contact person who can help facilitate this.

Cash flow forecasting

A cash flow is just that – the movement of money: ensuring your business stays in business. The money coming in each month needs to exceed what's going out.

Because of the way the typical business cycle works, you are likely to have to pay for materials, goods, etc. in order to satisfy an order. You will often have to pay up front – while the money you receive from the customer won't come in until much later.

A cash flow forecast, looking at your ins and outs on a month-by-month basis, is vital to flag up possible shortcomings and allow you to make provisions, perhaps in the form of a small loan, to ease you through. Forecast accurately, otherwise it won't be of much help. A spreadsheet programme such as OpenOffice or Excel will help.

Linked to overtrading is chasing turnover. The danger lies in accepting lots of contracts and being unable to fulfil them. It is not about the turnover you produce, it is about the profits you make and you will be unable to generate profits without cash to begin with. It's a cycle that needs to be monitored closely.

There are various sites online that can point you in the right direction when it comes to completing a cash flow forecast. Bytestart is one such site. The key is keeping it simple and accurate. Group costs and expenses together where you can to make the process easier to complete – and update it every week.

Remember, factoring and invoice discounting are options that can help you in the event that you know you're going to need help. You can offer discount to your clients if they pay up front, allowing you to pay for materials, or you can ask clients to pay 50% when confirming the order.

In brief, focus on turnover and you will keep busy – you will be a busy fool; focus instead on profit and not running out of cash. The quote *'Turnover is vanity, profit is sanity, but cash is king'* is attributed to 'various sources' and no wonder – your future success depends on it.

YOUR BUSINESS PLAN AND HOW TO PRESENT IT

Any entrepreneur wanting to survive in business has to have a vision, a plan.

A business plan is an essential tool for thriving and moving forward as a company. Make sure you have one. When you go on a car journey, if you're sensible you will have mapped your route. You know where you are. You know where you want to go and how you are going to get there. It is no different in business. A business plan will help you map out aspects such as funding, future plans, market trends, market size, accounting and cash flow … the list goes on.

It can be a disconcerting process, although it's essential if you want to succeed.

First, decide who you are writing your business plan for. It may be to attract investment from a bank or a business angel (as in the TV programme *Dragons' Den*), or it may be just a guideline document to keep you and your business on track, or it may be more of a sales and marketing-led document to tell potential customers what you do.

If you are requesting funding and are presenting to an investor, make sure you include how much you believe they will get in return for their investment, and within what time-scale.

At the beginning of the business plan include a summary. Rather like an introduction to a book, it should set out to excite the reader and get them to read on. In conjunction with this, draw up a brief overview of key benefits to be gleaned from your product or service and emphasize your USP, your unique selling point.

Areas to cover

Your business plan should include information about the size of the market you are targeting, and the predicted growth of that market over time. Spell out your knowledge of the competition, how you see your status in the industry and whether you can compete with the main players in your marketplace. Detail your professional contacts and have a section on your premises including licence details. Insurance, location information, accounting, finance, marketing, strategy for growth and managing staff should all be found in the best business plans. Get advice and make sure yours is up there with the best.

YOUR BUSINESS – START AND GROW YOUR BUSINESS

Your plan needs to be accurate, concise and an easy document for people to draw conclusions from. Make sure it has a professional feel, has no errors or spelling mistakes and is realistic in its predictions for how the company is going to grow. A PowerPoint presentation is, for once, a good idea – a good way of selling your business plan to would-be investors in a visual, compelling format.

The unique selling point of your business, the USP, is key. You need to explain to others why they should invest in you rather than elsewhere. Make sure they know what sort of opportunity they are getting, and that you are worth taking a risk on.

Include colour charts and spreadsheets and make sure your sections are headed up clearly, to include management, marketing, finance, etc.

As you may have seen on *Dragons' Den*, knowing the numbers is vitally important for those looking to invest. The numbers need to add up. A simple break-even chart (how much you must sell to cover your costs is your break-even figure) and a cash flow forecast should be included as well as sales projections. Be realistic in your assumptions. Perhaps an accountant can help you here.

Make sure that once the plan is drawn up, you use it and update it regularly. It is a living document that can help you on your path to success. Make sure, as with your cash flow and sales projections, you continually review and update it. How else will you know when you are close to completing your ultimate aim?

Into the dragons' den

At this point you may use your plan to invite investment from private investors. You will need to make a presentation and there is much more on presentations/speeches in Your Speaking (starting on page 189).

Note: as I mentioned above, you will need handouts and slides for a formal presentation to investors.

Be prepared for detailed scrutiny in the form of due diligence where the *truth* about your business *will* be uncovered, as your potential investors' accountants delve into your past accounts and order books.

KEEPING UP WITH TECHNOLOGY

Intelligent use of information technology is a must to achieve business success. It has changed the way we all work worldwide.

Flexibility is key. Emailing people after hours is expected and being available even when on holiday is seen as normal these days. Embrace the internet age, see what benefits you can gain from what's available, to help sustain and grow your business.

Once you're used to fast access at work, you'll want it on the road too. And here's where the latest wifi-enabled laptop could be handy, especially if you are often out on appointments (based around shopping centres, coffee shops, etc., countrywide).

A less cumbersome option is a smart phone, such as a Blackberry. These products integrate a mobile phone, personal organizer and internet access all in one handset.

You can do business updates, check your banking, use networking sites, make phone calls ... in fact, any number of things ... when you're on the move. As you grow your business and make more contacts, you are likely to be invited at some point to join a networking club of some sort. So it's not a surprise to learn that this can also be done virtually. Networking sites link together like-minded business people via the internet, providing you with potential leads, prospects, customers, ideas and suppliers without even leaving the office.

(For more on this, see Chapter 6 How to Master Cyberspace (like a ten-year-old), page 71.)

MARKETING AND PUBLICITY

Spend time marketing your product.

Position your business to prospective buyers to help generate sales. That is, essentially, what marketing is. Keep taking any action you can think of to get your company noticed. Make sure you keep a track on marketing activity; be scientific in your approach to assessing the effectiveness of various marketing methods. You can invest in advertising, website optimization, networking, newsletters, emails, direct mail, telesales and DVDs, which can all help get your business out in the public eye.

Think about where your customers and clients go and how they buy, then make sure a marketing message about you and your company is there for them to see.

Getting publicity often involves generating a story around you or your product or service. This can be something papers, magazines and websites are willing to feature, providing you with a form of free advertising. Make sure you include a link to buy at the end of your feature or article (either direct or via a retail partner).

SALES

Marketing leads to sales – that's the plan, anyway! Once your marketing efforts have generated you a list of prospects, your job is to turn them into sales. This will be done in one of three ways. If you are in mail order, selling over the internet, have a clear process in place, from prospect through to sale. It would start with sending more information about your product, along with a clear money-back guarantee, and it would continue with clear communications at every stage. Your customer will only buy once they are confident they will receive what they expect.

On the other hand, if you are selling services, you would probably meet with your customer, either in person or on a video conference call.

Remember you are not just selling your product or service; you are selling the benefits of it to your customer. Clearly articulate what these are, and why your product or service is better than your competitors'. Your unique selling point is crucial to sales and is a powerful marketing tool. Salespeople need to listen as well as sell – use empathy as a sales tool; it works. It is vital to find out what your potential customers need. Now explain how your product can meet those needs. It may be more expensive than others so you'll need to explain why. Turn objections into advantages and tell them what your other clients have got from the product which they too could utilize.

Close the deal as early as possible, and if the customer isn't ready, ask them *when* they will need the product. Don't say *if!* Finally, when the order is in, thank them.

Now make it happen. You know you have it in you to make it work. Just do it.

EMPLOYING STAFF

Think twice before employing as it can be easier and less risky to buy some skills in on a contractual basis as they are needed, avoiding the commitment and the responsibility of taking on employees when the future of your business is unknown.

If you find you need employees, remember that people are your business. The wrong people can cause you great harm. So when you meet someone for the first time in an interview, be prepared to ask the right questions, to see examples of their work, and take up all references to help you ascertain whether they are suitable.

Consider whether it's a full-time or part-time position, and advertise on the basis of the new skills you require, having drawn up a suitable job description. It is vital to include skills, experience and knowledge while highlighting job tasks, title and where it will be based.

A recruitment agency, although expensive, might be preferable and would save you time. Also, consider including a probationary period in the employment contract. Once a candidate has been found, do some pre-planning on the interview process. What can you offer an employee, for instance? Remember, it's a two-way street.

There are plenty of websites offering you advice on interviewing technique and it would be wise to do some research.

Employment law

There's a lot to know about the legalities of employing people. It's the main area where small businesses either wittingly or unwittingly fall foul of the law. New laws, and there are many, are introduced all the time and can be baffling. Do not ask applicants for personal details to begin with and seek advice on the way you set up your premises for interview, such as for wheelchair access, lighting and so on.

What pension provisions will you furnish? What job-related benefits will be available immediately and which will be phased in over time? This information should be made available to the applicant so they can assess their own suitability.

An employee must have a written statement of employment, normally within two months. Think of the things you need to cover in the document. Company name, employee's name, date of commencement of employment, job title, address of workplace – all these things need to be included. How much are you going to pay them? What are their hours of work? What holiday days are available?

Under 'separate advice', detail sickness, injury and sick pay details, period of employment, notice periods, details of overseas employment, pension details and disciplinary and grievance procedures. Bonuses, commission and obligations for an annual salary review should also be mentioned.

Management roles should include issues such as confidentiality, fidelity, including adequate restrictions once they've left your business, periods of notice required and gardening leave, if appropriate.

Consider making the period of the employment contract last for a year with a clause about when it is to be renewed as this will allow scope to discontinue employment or to change terms.

LOCATION, LOCATION, LOCATION

Home or office? Your decision is vital. A sole trader on the internet most of the time will get away with working from home. If you can, set up your home office in a separate space to your living space – in its own room, or a building out in the garden, for instance. Beware the perils of not being able to switch off from your business if you aren't actually travelling to and from an office or premises.

This can be difficult, but a balanced life is important to your energy levels.

Retail premises require a prime location if you can afford the lease.

Many companies have gone down the virtual office route, which provides an office address and telephone answering service that serves a number of companies. You would either collect your mail from the serviced office, or have it sent on to you, and these service company providers would have different phone numbers coming into one building, each one allocated to one of the companies they support.

However, choose such a company with great care. With some it is obvious they know nothing about you or your company when someone phones. Get to know the people in the service company and build up a trusted relationship with them and you will get a better service.

You can rent premises if you are confident enough in your future plans for growth, but be aware that this can be the most costly option.

Whichever option you select, you will need to meet your customers in a prestigious, professional location. I recommend joining a local Institute of Directors (www.iod.com) or meeting in hotels. If you do use a hotel, try to use the same one again and build up a trusted relationship so that you are known and treated well.

Once you've decided on an office type, fix your budget, remembering to include overhead costs and capital costs, such as any equipment you may need. You could rent certain items to start off with, until you can afford to buy.

Think about transport links for your employees when considering location too, as well as nearby shops and amenities. Consider the physical size of the firm too, in terms of space required, including any plans to expand. Consulting commercial property agents will benefit you.

Share what you know. Don't hide things. Find out what you need to know by communicating. It's the only way.

PLUS THREE

There are three additional key factors to consider, over and above the essentials mentioned here.

1 Remember that the person who starts a company is rarely the best person to grow it, which calls for different skills and a fresh approach. As a founder, be prepared to stand back and take a different role after your company reaches a certain size.

2   Make sure you surround yourself with experts that you trust in the following key areas – the law, accountancy and banking/finance.

3   Start your business with a clear exit plan. Are you going to sell, float on a stock exchange, or leave it for your children or other relatives to take over? If you are going to sell, start planning now by speaking with your banking expert; if you aim to float, start planning now with your lawyer; and if you are going to leave it for someone else, start planning now with your accountant.

Finally, in a chapter that has been of necessity 'information overload', please update your will, so that you know what will happen to your company after you die.

That's quite enough. No story on this one, other than yours. As you start your business and you progress on your journey, keep a record, a journal, and always record your achievements, as well as your plans.

YOUR THREE KEY ACTIONS

- Read this chapter again, and make a checklist of 'to do' items.
- Be aware of your legal responsibilities as a company director.
- Surround yourself with good advisers in law, accountancy and banking. They will serve you well.

The Journey of Hindsight continues at VII Your Book – 20 How to Have It Published (while staying sane) on page 251.

The Journey of Misadventure continues at IV Your Warning! – 12 How to Never Be Found Out (by 'reality') on page 145.

HOW TO UNLOCK THE 'HOLY GRAIL' OF FAST BUSINESS GROWTH

'Conformity is the jailer of freedom and the enemy of growth.'

John F. Kennedy

SUMMARY

Get 'back to business': from the moment you start, keep returning to why your business exists and what it's there to do. Identify your cause, your mission statement, what you stand for. Unlock the assets you already have, make fast decisions and serve your customers – they are why you exist. Oh yes, and *get paid!*

As an organization, there is one way you can be sure to accelerate through any economic times, one thing that will stand you in a very strong competitive position.

GET BACK TO BUSINESS

Just had a great business idea? Tomorrow, when the planning all kicks off, make sure you *get back to business*.

Out celebrating with your colleagues after starting the company? Great. Tomorrow, headaches and all, *get back to business*.

Planning your company? As you plan, *get back to business*.

This sounds simple – but that does not make it easy. It is the key factor that at some stage, people (organizations) forget.

Whether you are just starting out, or you are a small to medium-sized company (SME), whether you are an entrepreneur, or you have been trading for many years – you are far, far more likely to achieve accelerated business success when you keep at the forefront of your mind exactly why you started the business in the first place.

As your organization grows, beware complexity for complexity's sake! When complexities arrive, things can get very fuzzy. Be clear about where you are going by dropping business jargon in favour of language a ten-year-old could understand. It will serve you well.

Forgive me quoting from one of my own books!

> *Go into any new company, one that is just starting out. Witness the enthusiasm, energy and excitement as the founders discuss their dreams, shape their future and make their plans a positive reality. Feel the culture of a new project at its launch – a new team comes together for the first time, full of hope and expectation at the success ahead of them. Experience a company as it grows fast; see the ideas, instinct and imagination flow through everyone involved, like a collective heartbeat of inspiration. It is a healing process, providing an atmosphere of certainty in the destiny that is being shaped by their constructive forces.*
>
> *Go into any large company, one that has been established for a while. Introduce a management initiative, call it total quality anything, or continuous improvement, or worse still, business process re-engineering, then stand back and watch. The blame starts slowly at first, then grows, fast. It eats its way through an organisation, freezing new ideas, initiative and action in its wake. It is like a virus of negativity. War breaks out as everyone focuses on saving costs, avoiding failure, and rooting out anyone who dares to make a mistake. It is a harming process, providing an atmosphere of inevitability in the disaster that is being shaped by destructive forces.*
>
> *The Naked Leader*, Capstone, 2002

These words are as true today as they were ten years ago when I first wrote them. As your company grows, don't lose the magic, the passion, or the reason that you started the business in the first place. If you do, every day will become a chore, and it simply won't be any fun anymore.

WHAT TO DO?

Getting back to business means applying common sense and learning the lessons from the last economic downturn, when too many organizations simply did not learn from their past mistakes. Make sure you don't embark on such a waste of time, money, energy and resources. Reapply the things that worked, and avoid the things that didn't work.

You will probably know, by now, that success, as defined by you, does not happen by accident – when you, your teams and projects, and your organization are successful, 'clues' are left behind, and you can build on and grow the structure.

That structure is based on:

1   Knowing where you want to go.
2   Knowing where you are now.
3   Knowing what you have to do, to get to where you want to go.
4   Doing it.

Let's look in more detail at what each of these 'cornerstones' of good business sense involves.

KNOWING WHERE YOU WANT TO GO

Business has a powerful role to play in, and a responsibility towards, transforming our world, and helping future generations inherit a society of mutual respect, enlightenment and peace. Make your business both great and good.

Encourage trust, ethics and integrity in all things and at all times – with corporate, social and even world responsibility at the heart of your agenda. Make sure everyone within your organization knows what their role is in helping make the pledges a reality, the dream become true.

How?

Firstly, and fundamentally – have a *cause*. And put it before making *cash*.

If there is one line in this whole book that summarizes why this is not about simply making money, it is this:

Put your cause before making your cash – you will make more cash as a result.

Your cause is what you stand for, what you are putting back into the community, the world, and how you are making a difference.

And if those words sound like I am asking you to be a 'do-gooder' – well, yes, I am.

A cause brings together all of your corporate and social responsibility initiatives. It can be something closely aligned with your business objectives, or something completely unrelated, but it must reflect what you feel strongly about.

Examples of corporate causes are:

In 2007, Marks & Spencer announced its intention to become carbon neutral by 2012. This is part of the company's blueprint for success.

www.marksandspencer.com

In 2005, HSBC was the first bank and FTSE100 company to become carbon neutral.

www.hsbc.com

Boots partners with the National Health Service which reflects its core business interests whilst establishing a 'feel-good factor'. It's a partnership approach to corporate community investment which has made a positive impact on its business.

www.boots.com

And in smaller, more entrepreneurial companies:

Asap Photographic Services, a Belgian photographic company, has built its business around a sustainable development model that includes a system to purify the water that is used in the photographic development process.

www.asap-fotolab.be

The Island Hotels Group in Malta demonstrated concern for their community environment by modifying their approach to demolishing and rebuilding the Golden Sands Hotel.

www.islandhotels.com

The Pixel Foundry in Wales is a small TV and video production company who encourage other hi-tech small businesses to share offices in the village to 'benefit from the inter-trading and collaboration opportunities that exist'.

www.pixelfoundry.co.uk

What's your *cause*?

What do you stand for?

What are your values?

What difference are you here to make, and for who?

'I keep going by recognizing what I have achieved, not what I have not.'
Caroline Hayward, managing director, the Chairman's Network, www.chairmansnetwork.com

Focus on what you want, not what you don't want – each and every day, in everything that you think, say and do.

Why?

Your mind is structured to automatically take you in the direction of whatever you think about most. So, focus on what you want and you will automatically start going towards what you want – focus on what you don't, and you will automatically start going towards what you don't want.

Focus on the numbers

As a company, of any size, you will have a relentless focus on the numbers, i.e. profit and loss – where you are each and every day; where you plan to be next week, month and year; and your overall numbers target to achieve your business endgame.

So, know the numbers inside out, upside down and back to front – and know what they mean, using this question:

Which parts of the company are making profit, which parts are not?

Profit is not a 'dirty' word, or a 'clean' word – it is the *only* word!

I feel sorry for companies who make a good profit and demonstrate good business results only to be criticized by the media which focuses on bonuses and fat-cat CEOs. The same papers then have an even bigger 'axe to grind' when companies make a loss and have to make redundancies.

That's not half as sorry as I feel for the companies who go out of business every working day – every statistic hiding personal distress, unpaid creditors, and lessons learned all too late.

Knowing where you want to go means knowing where you want to end up. Have a clear idea what your 'endgame' is. Here are some possible outcomes:

- Sell your business. There are companies that specialize in facilitating such sales. Speak with your bank for initial advice.
- Float your business on a public stock exchange. To do this you need professional advice from an accountant or solicitor.
- Stand back and play a different role. For companies to grow, the person who started them is not often the best person to grow them.
- Pass your business on to your children. Watch out for tax implications, and make sure they really want it!

There is one critical exception to always returning to why you started the business in the first place, and that is if your business discovers a new, faster way to grow, a new reason for existence, or a new or extended cause.

> Nokia began as a riverside paper mill in south-western Finland and became a global telecommunications leader.
>
> Viagra (sildenafil citrate) was originally marketed to reduce high blood pressure, and then they noticed an interesting side effect in the patients.
>
> Lucozade started as an energy drink in health recovery and is now a world leader in the sports market.

KNOWING WHERE YOU ARE NOW

Strip away the hype, the jargon and mystery surrounding your organization. Deliver radical simplicity – clear, concise and compelling actions and futures. Reduce red tape and processes, and agree an agenda in which every team, project and activity directly relates to you achieving your objectives.

How?

Ensure clear ownership and accountability of every action, project and process – that is, *one single person* needs to own and be accountable for an action's completion (they do not have to do all the work themselves, just ensure the work gets done). Don't be tempted to give an action, project or process more than one owner – or it won't get done. Your staff need clear roles, and they also need to know what everyone else's role is. As you grow, this will become more difficult; as you grow, this will become ever more critical.

Make sure that everything you do helps you get closer to your endgame or takes your business forward. If it doesn't, stop doing it. Unless you enjoy doing it, of course, in which case go lock yourself in a room, carry on working in isolation at your really exciting project, and enjoy yourself (you will of course have resigned from your company at this point).

Transform communications. Make sure that everyone knows who to go to, or where to go, to find out what they need to know, *and* that they feel they can do this without fear or favour. Bring the truth into the room, so you focus on the issues that matter. From time to time, every company will experience issues you prefer not to deal with, sticky situations you would rather ignore or difficult conversations you would rather leave until tomorrow. Don't be tempted to let these things fester. I call it 'bringing the truth into the room', acknowledging the sometimes difficult truths that hold the key to your business success.

Play to people's strengths and passions as much as possible, and avoid using the word 'competencies' (for fear of people falling asleep).

KNOWING WHAT YOU HAVE TO DO, TO GET TO WHERE YOU WANT TO GO

Organizations don't change, only people do, and they will only do so for one reason, and one reason alone: if they want to. Don't change for the sake of it – and above all, don't change what has worked in the past. There are no straightforward answers any more. Best practice doesn't work because what works in one organization may not work in another. So it comes down to the choices and decisions we make each and every day.

How?

If anyone tells you that your organization needs to 'change,' ask this: 'Change what?' Get a context for change, and you stop talking about change for its own sake; you start to focus on choice instead. Learn from what you do well. Too many bigger companies focus on learning from what they do wrong. That often leads them to protect what they have, which in turn leads to a lack of innovation, action and profit. Do not join them.

Ideas and choices

When considering what you need to do, start with as many choices, as many ideas, as possible.

My top seven ways to unleash ideas, imagination and innovation are:

1 Believe there are new ideas out there (otherwise you won't have any).
2 Bring your bubbly, emotional, full-on personality to work and encourage others to do the same.
3 Recruit crazy people with crazy ideas, or at least network with them.
4 Open up to other points of view than your own – read more than one book!
5 Listen without your ego – do not judge, only notice.
6 Go talk to a school and ask them for ideas – young people never think 'outside of the box' because they don't know there is a box in the first place.
7 Go with your gut feel, your instinct.

Narrowing down the choices

Having so many choices does not make life any easier (I am old enough to remember when you could walk into a coffee shop, ask for a drink, and get one, without having to choose the cup size, the type of coffee bean, the milk...).

Now you have to narrow these down as quickly as possible, to get to a true decision which is going to work for you and your business. Encourage this by ensuring time for open and free conversation in any meeting. Moving the 'any other business' agenda point to the top of your meeting schedule is a good move too. That's where the really important stuff often gets discussed, only to be cut short when you run out of time. *Open and honest conversation* means just that. If you do not contribute during this part of the meeting (i.e. say what you think, make a proposal on what to do, or raise what has to be raised), then you lose your right to speak on that subject. Have a time limit on this – it will actually encourage people to bring the truth into the room, and get to the point quicker.

Conclude with the big decision(s) that you have to take – state them so everyone is clear. Make true decisions, ones that you all buy into, about *what* you want to achieve and *how you are going to get there*. In other words, by making a true decision *you close off all other possible outcomes*. The biggest single disabler to organizations of every size is their inability to make a true decision.

HOW TO MAKE A TRUE DECISION

Agree in advance that any and all decisions you make in a meeting will be 'true' so that you won't keep raising the same issues every time you meet and you won't keep going round in circles.

Agree how a decision will be made, before the discussion takes place. Here are some approaches:

1 A straight vote which can be a secret ballot if the issue is a sensitive one (when it may affect the outcome of the vote by being open).
2 If it is a specialist area owned by a specific person, that person decides.
3 Pure seniority: the chairman holds the final decision.
4 If the decision comes down to a choice between two close outcomes, between option A or B – toss a coin.
5 Go with your 'gut feeling': remember your gut feel is a combination of all of your knowledge and experience to date, and can serve you well when making critical, true decisions.

Finally, ensure the business is not dependent on any one person. Realize that as the company grows, you may need a new manager, a new leader. The person with the initial idea may not be the best person to grow the company, who in turn may not be the best person to sell it.

DO IT!

This is about taking action, and being persistent as you do so. Doing it means just that, not thinking, not talking – doing.

In the wider context of your life, this is covered in Chapter 1 on page 3. In the context of your business, it comes down to...

Customers

Your customers are why you exist. Without them, you have no business, no organization. They must be at the top of your priorities, in the eyes, minds and actions of all of your people. Your number one aim is to attract, retain and delight your customers so that they come back for more. Ensure your organizational processes, charts and roles reflect this. If your structure is vertical, put customers at the top. If it is horizontal, put customers end to end. And put true decision-making power where it belongs – with the people serving your customers.

How?

Make sure that everything that you do is wrapped around your customers – ask the question, 'How does what we are doing, or planning to do, or thinking about doing, directly benefit our customers?' Your customers will make their buying decisions for emotional reasons, and it will always come down to a desire to move away from pain (the main driver), towards pleasure (a close second). What pain does your product or service or offering reduce or, ideally, eliminate? What pleasure does your product, or service, or offering increase or, ideally, make permanent? Customers want you to make decisions there and then, not to come back to them later, so maximize the decisions that your people are able to make on the phone, in reception and directly to customers. If you have to go back to the customer at some later point, make sure the person doing so takes personal ownership and follows through.

When a customer writes to you or emails you – reply. Do this one thing consistently and you will be among a very small proportion of companies!

When something goes wrong, it is one of your biggest op-portunities to impress your customers. After all, at this point their expectations are very low (so you can easily exceed them) and their emotions are very high (so they are more likely to buy). This is not a flippant comment – respect their feelings, listen to their needs, and then make an offer that exceeds their expectations. Have lemons and small bottles of lemonade on hand in your office. As customers complain, grasp the lemon. When you have resolved the issue, take a sip of lemonade.

YOUR THREE KEY ACTIONS

- Focus on your business fundamentals from day one.
- Have a cause, something you stand for.
- Your customers are the reason you exist. Delight them.

The Journey of Hindsight continues at II Your Brand – 6 How to Master Cyberspace (like a ten-year-old) on page 71.

The Journey of Misadventure continues at IV Your Warning! – 10 How to Make the Big Decision (Don't give up your day job just yet) on page 131.

'In business you get what you want by giving other people what they want.'

Alice MacDougall, US businesswoman

SUMMARY
Sell what others want to buy (that reduces or removes a 'pain' they have and/or gives them a 'pleasure'). Have your proposition down to a clear 'hook' (3 seconds), 'line' (7 seconds) and 'sinker' (21 seconds). And *get paid* – a sale is not a sale until the money is in your bank account.

SELL WHAT OTHERS WANT TO BUY

In times of growth and times of recession, one principle stays the same:

People will always buy goods or services that they perceive they need from other people that they trust, at a fair price that meets or exceeds their expectations.

What do others want to buy?

Buying decisions are emotional (we stack the logic up, afterwards), and they come down to two main drivers: things that propel us towards pleasure or away from pain. Think about what pain your business can help remove, and what pleasure it can help make happen, more often.

For example, a company may be experiencing 'pain' because of costs being too high, a lack of customers, website not getting enough hits, an unclear strategy, morale being low, change programmes not working, etc. These are results or issues they want to collectively move away from.

Alternatively, you may be able to help a company that wants more 'pleasure', which may include higher profit, increased morale, more loyal customers, winning more awards, higher global recognition, etc. These are results or issues they want to collectively move closer to.

In entrepreneurial terms, there are four needs that have been around for years, and will continue to be for some time:

1 *Influence* – Will your product or service give the buyer greater personal influence in their team or organization?
2 *Answers* – Does your business answer a specific, real and painful problem being faced by the buyer – and in solving their challenge, will it make the buyer look a hero?
3 *Time* – Will your product or service save the buyer time – their most precious commodity? Or at least appear to save them time?
4 *Friends* – Will your idea help the buyer be better known, build their network or gain access to a wider number of people?

Sell it

This is where you turn your big idea, the centrepiece of everything in this book, into a killer proposition that sells itself.

No small promise.

How?

Write out your big idea, in language a ten-year-old would understand. Identify what exact pain (problem) will be overcome and what exact pleasure (benefits) will be achieved as a result of your big idea. Combine the two. Make sure that your big idea appeals *both* to a problem being sorted *and* to an opportunity being achieved.

The killer part – Add the consequences of not doing something about the problem, so you end up with a three-part 'killer proposition'.

1   A problem that it will resolve (pain).
2   The big idea that will sort it and deliver an exact result (pleasure).
3   The consequences of not doing something about it (pain).

Write down your target market and the exact problems that your big idea will resolve. Your sale is now made in a 3-second 'hook', a 7-second 'line' and a 21-second 'sinker'.

With so much information, knowledge and so many choices out there, our attention spans are short and you have to grab your potential customer's attention very fast, or you may have lost them forever.

Hook – 3 seconds – tick, tock and tick

Have a single line that summarizes your killer proposition – your aim is to appeal to emotional interest here. Over the years we have had:

Domino's Pizza – 'Fresh hot pizza delivered in thirty minutes or less, or it's free.'

Federal Express – 'When it absolutely, positively, has to be there.'

Master Foods – 'A Mars a day helps you work, rest and play.'

Line – 7 seconds

Now that you have their attention, you must keep it, by sharing what you do and how that will benefit your customers. Three of the best 7-second, 'line' statements I have heard from the business-to-business market are listed below. In each example, note that the first sentence could also be the 3-second hook and used as such:

'We tell the story of your company – through the eyes of your people. We have done this for companies all over the world, with remarkable results.'

www.the-storytellers.com

'With Crunch you save money, become more tax efficient and pay less in accountancy fees. And because you pay just one low monthly fee, you get the benefits of professional accountants without big bills. Are you ready to change the way you do your accounts, forever?'

www.crunch.co.uk

'The design and implementation of a robust IT infrastructure is critical to an organization's success. As such, choosing the right technology partner is the first step in ensuring that your IT infrastructure meets your core business objectives.'

www.arcomit.co.uk

And finally, the 21-second sinker

This is where you make an offer, a call to action – and in your 21 seconds you make it clear what has to happen next.

The emotional sale was made in the 3-second hook and 7-second line; now, with the sinker, the thing to agree on is what happens next. My suggested words – in person, on the phone or by email, would be your own variation of: *It would be useful if we could meet for an hour, so we can share with you ways that you can move closer to achieving [insert what they want to achieve].*

Or: *It would be useful if we could meet for an hour, so we can share with you ways that you can avoid [insert what they don't want to achieve].*

Or: *It would be useful if we could meet for an hour, so we can discuss how we can help each other.*

Have some customer references in hand, to offer if you feel appropriate, and then ask directly for the meeting: *'I can meet on Thursday morning or next Monday afternoon.'*

Then pause again and gauge reaction, always remembering that your aim here is to get a meeting – so you can form a trusted relationship.

This is not a hard sell.

Customers *hate* to be sold to – but they *love* to buy. So keep giving them freedom and choices and let them drive the agenda.

Now, you have the first meeting.

- **Be prepared**. Know your customer.
  Business to Consumer (B2C). Why do they come into your shop/garage/workshop? Why are they a regular customer (or not)? Know their name and something significant about them.
  With Business to Business (B2B), get to know your client's company better than they know it themselves. Get familiar with the challenges they are facing and the pressures they are under, and make it your business to provide solutions.
- **Be emotional**. 'Pain' and 'pleasure' are both experiences people have – find out what experiences your potential customers will have by asking 'So what?' of yourself at every stage. We have that to offer – 'So what?' – so that means you retain your better staff – 'So what?' – by retaining your best leaders, you are more likely to be successful – 'So what?' Be really tough on yourself by asking this question over and over again for all of your products, services and offerings.
- **Be honest**. If you cannot meet any of the needs being discussed, say so, suggest or recommend someone else if you can, and end the meeting there and then. You will be remembered forever – and called again when the time is right.
- **Be personal**. People buy from people, so take time to get to know the person in front of you – they will make the decision. To buy from you they must trust and respect you. To buy lots from you they must also like you. End of story.
- **Be quiet**. Listen, and ask questions. Let the other person talk about their favourite subject, themselves. Answer their main question – 'What's in it for me?' Read their body language like a book.
- **Be certain**. To make any sale you have to exude confidence, without being arrogant. You have to be bold, while being humble. Prove the faith you have in your own product or service by offering risk-sharing solutions, such as staged payments.

- **Be clever**. Make it easy to buy, and to evaluate once bought. Time is a cherished commodity, so don't take up too much of it. Make it absolutely clear what happens next, and make the process easy for your buyer.

(Abridged from *The Naked Leader Experience*)

DELIVER

Business is not just about making money, it is about delighting your customers. Making money is the by-product. And you will delight your customers by following through and delivering on what you promise.

Follow through: deliver on your promise.

Follow through: be seen to deliver on your agreement.

Follow through: if something goes wrong, make it right, and then more than right.

Every customer-supplier dispute, the loss of a customer, a fall-out with a client, a decision by a potential customer not to come to you, or return to you – they all come down to one thing: an actual, or perceived (same thing), broken promise.

Make sure you deliver and follow through on your deals, your agreements and your promises – always.

Say what you mean and mean what you say; mean what you say and say what you mean.

And if something goes wrong, that prevents you from fulfilling your promises, then you have a lemon on your hands. It is your job to turn that lemon into lemonade. Remember that when things go wrong, your customers have very low expectations of you, and very high emotions.

Take ownership, be honest about what happened and apologize.

We decided to host a very exclusive chief executive officers (CEOs) dinner at an expensive London venue. This was a big investment for us – our outcome was to widen our network of CEOs. The invitations were hand designed and written, the CEOs carefully selected, and the envelopes were for the personal attention of the CEOs' personal assistant, by name.

We sent out 50, and our target was to secure six for the dinner.

What could go wrong?

Well, and I almost can't write this … well, we (I take full ownership) did not weigh the envelope properly, and the standard first class stamp we put on the front was not enough to cover postage – it was short by two pence.

In the UK, when this happens, the person it is being delivered to is asked if they are prepared to make up the difference, to accept the letter.

I think you get the picture.

My partner got the first call of complaint – from a CEO (PAs will always share such stories with their bosses) – and she and I sat in a room to work out how to turn this almighty 'lemon' into 'lemonade'. Well, it was light when we first sat down; it was dark by the time we stood up again!

We went through the full range of options – sending flowers for each PA (over the top), or an email of apologies (under the top) – and eventually we decided that I would personally phone each one of the 50, to apologize.

You know those days when you wake up, and you have to make one difficult phone call? I woke up having to make 50 of them!

Well, what was the very worst that could happen? None of them would come to our event. As things stood at this stage, none of them was coming anyway.

So we were already facing the worst-case scenario…

Now, in normal circumstances, how many of 50 CEOs that I had never spoken with, would I get through to? I would guess, none (hence the invitation). The number I got through to on this occasion – 26.

Twenty-six!

Fifty-two per cent!!!

The PAs, who I also apologized to, were positively salivating to put me through (a lamb to the slaughter) – and I spoke one to one with 26 new CEOs. Not only was I able to apologize in person, I was able to pitch to get them to accept the invitation and the dinner went ahead – yes, a hugely successful dinner went ahead, which subsequently led on to the new business we were seeking.

Please, I am not suggesting you create a lemon just for the sake of it, although it is interesting how people pull together in a crisis. I am suggesting that when they happen, you turn them to your advantage.

GET PAID

Unless and until you get paid you have not made a sale.

A true 'sale' is not a lead, a meeting, the signing of a contract, the carrying out of work, the follow-up meetings. A true 'sale' only happens when you *get paid*.

As the character Rod Tidwell says in the film *Jerry Maguire*, by Cameron Crowe, *'Show me the money.'*

If you think that the person in your team or organization who is responsible for credit control is a 'back office' function, go and fill a bucket with cold water. Now place your own head in the water and stay there until you are convinced.

Invoice as soon as the goods are received or the event is completed, and have clear payment terms, e.g. payment within 14 days. On the 15th day phone the company up *and* write to them. Get a single point of contact.

Most companies will pay you according to their own terms (more often 28 days, plus). If this is fine by you, then great. Still call and write as above.

Some companies will take longer to pay; these will tend to be bigger companies and there are some recurring names who do this as a matter of course. This has got to stop, and it is time for small companies and entrepreneurs to get together to put collective pressure on these companies – visit www.nakedleader. com to share your experiences and join forces with other entrepreneurs.

And a message to the big companies that do this as a matter of course – you are threatening the survival many small companies and this practice has to stop. And stop it will.

Paid how much?

How much do you charge for what you offer and for what you do?

The quick answer is: what other people (individuals or organizations) will pay.

The more considered answer is what other people will pay, that will bring you the income that you need to achieve your targets. I know many excellent speakers and entrepreneurs who are very much in demand and could easily charge more. Equally, I know people who hold out for a much larger amount and do not get as much work as they need.

It is a balance between what you know you are worth (based on the value that you bring) set against the income you need to at one end make a living and at the other make a million.

Look at the competition within your sector, and find out how much others charge. Actual amounts will be difficult to discover; however, people and services will tend to fall into one of three categories: low, average and high.

Overall, my advice is set a fair rate for what you sell and what you do, and provide clear, measurable value for money.

Finally, a big question – should you ever do work for free?

Yes, absolutely, but draw a line at the amount of time you give for free. We do free events for The Prince's Trust, for local charities and in schools. We set a number of days a year to do this. We do this to put something back, to reach people who would not otherwise hear our messages and because The Prince's Trust is our charity of choice.

The biggest challenge of doing stuff free is actually less to do with not earning money, and more to do with the value you will be perceived to offer! People are less likely to turn up at a free event than one they paid for. So if you do a charity event, suggest that people pay to attend, and the money goes to the charity, rather than attending free and the charity making their money on, for example, an auction.

From bedroom to boardroom

The internet is the second Industrial Revolution, with even bigger potential consequences, and you can make money from it if you have a broadband connection.

To sell successfully online, apply the same principles we have already covered: see what others want to buy, sell for more than it cost you, and do it at a price that represents fair value.

You can read many books, and hear much advice, that tells you that selling online is different – that was the problem faced in the so-called 'dotcom' boom of the early years of the 21st century.

Then people realized: Hang on, the net is just a new, powerful route to market.

So, read again:

To sell successfully online, apply the same principles we have already covered – see what others want to buy, sell for more than it cost you, and do it at a price that represents fair value.

Selling online has four major advantages:

1 You can start up for a fraction of the cost.
2 You can work from home (prestigious business addresses are dead).
3 You can trial and error: what you sell, how you market, and how you sell.
4 Your business is open 24/7 – so you make money while you sleep.

Build trust online, and sell even more. Examples of what you could sell:

• Physical products
• Information or knowledge, often in downloadable form
• Advertising
• Your own services as a coach/speaker/consultant
• Online networking/membership of online communities

FIVE DOTCOMS THAT FAILED

I would argue that all of these companies failed for one of three reasons:

1 They were over-valued because they were online businesses. It was believed during the dotcom bubble that just being present online was enough be incredibly successful.
2 Their business model would not work away from the net, so it would not work on the net.
3 They were run by people who knew how to spend, instead of how to earn – this was not entirely their own fault, as they were well trained by over-zealous venture capitalists who were falling over themselves to invest millions in start-ups.

Rest in peace

- Boo.com spent $188 million in just six months in an attempt to create a global online fashion store. The company went bankrupt in May 2000.
- eToys: this retailer's share price went from $80 reached during its IPO in May 1999 to less than $1 when it declared bankruptcy in February 2001.
- Freeinternet.com filed for bankruptcy after losing $19 million in 1999 on revenues of less than $1 million.
- Webvan (1999–2001), an online grocery company (grocery, small margins), spent over $375 million dollars and went bust inside two years, with 2000 people losing their jobs.
- Pets.com (1998–2000) spent massively on advertising including at the US Super-Bowl. The company could not get over the lack of demand for its products when customers could buy and collect cat food locally without paying for shipping.

It's very easy for me and others to be pious about these examples; that is not the aim here. The aim is to say this to you: if you have a business model that works offline, it may work faster and better online, *and* you should do the same online as you would offline – form trusted relationships with your customers, sell them what they want at a fair price and follow through.

YOUR THREE KEY ACTIONS

- Identify in your market what causes your customers pain and what takes them towards pleasure.
- Have an amazing, magnetic, killer proposition, then deliver it.
- Get paid for what you do.

The Journey of Hindsight ends at V Your Secrets – 14 How to Help Others (and change the world for good) on page 167.

The Journey of Misadventure also ends at V Your Secrets – 14 How to Help Others (and change the world for good) on page 167.

IV

YOUR WARNING!
AVOID THE PITFALLS
THAT I DIDN'T

'If you put off everything until you're sure of it, you'll get nothing done.'

Norman Vincent Peale

SUMMARY

You don't have to resign your day job to start making money. If your job is made redundant, turn a difficult situation to your advantage. Otherwise, you can start your company while still in employment. If and when you do leave, choose and plan your timing and exit carefully.

In 1998 I did one of the craziest things I have ever done: I resigned from a safe, secure and well-paid job with Cornhill Insurance.

I mean, what was I thinking? I must have been completely mad.

Yes, I wanted to get out of corporate life; yes, I wanted to be master of my own destiny; but inspiring/meaningless phrases like that mean nothing when you have a family who depend on you to put food on their plates.

If you want to write a book, you don't have to give up your day job. If you want to be a professional speaker, you can train for that within your present company; and if you want to start your own business, especially online, you don't have to give up your primary source of income until you know it is a success.

On the other hand, if you have decided to run a business that needs your full-time time, energy and presence, I strongly recommend that you don't leave your existing organization until you have everything planned and in place... unless of course you are made redundant.

Let's deal with the 'R' word first, and how you can turn an often very difficult experience to your advantage.

REDUNDANCY

Being made redundant used to have a negative stigma. Nowadays it is much more common, with few such connotations. The challenge with being made redundant is to remain positive, and to see it as the start, not the end.

Always remember this: it is the job that is made redundant, not the person.

Know this at every level. It may feel personal, and it may even be because the person being made redundant did not get on with the right people, but it is always the job that is made redundant.

How can any human being be 'redundant?'

From helpless to helpful

If you are made redundant, no matter how you may be feeling:

- Take ownership of your situation – that means taking responsibility for what happens next. Ask yourself this: is there anyone out there in poorer or more challenging circumstances than you, who has gone on to secure a better job? If the answer is yes, then it is more than possible.
- It doesn't matter how few jobs there are out there, the only way to get one is to apply for them, and keep doing so until you get one. Rejection letters are never personal, so for every one that arrives, apply for two more jobs.
- Perhaps now is the time to work for yourself, to put your big idea to the test and start making things happen! Fate has intervened; your job has been made redundant. Now use your redundancy money to fund phase one of your business and start on your Naked Millionaire journey.

Focus on your desired outcome rather than your perceived problem. Do this by changing the three most negative thoughts that you may be having:

1   From focusing on what you don't want to *focusing on what you do want*.
2   From things being done to you to *things being done by you*.
3   From what you have discovered you can't do to *discovering what you can do*.

These are the three mindset changes that have the greatest, and the fastest positive impact.

Whether you have a deep, burning desire to start your own business at some stage in your life, or circumstances have forced you to consider it right now, answer this one question, without hesitation:

Would working for yourself excite you, at any level?

If your immediate, instinctive answer to this is 'yes' or 'maybe', then give it some further consideration.

And you will not be alone – during the recent global recession, more people started working for themselves than in any equivalent period before. Such one-person, small, entrepreneurial companies are becoming the lifeblood of economies throughout the world.

So, if you are in paid employment right now, and would like to work for yourself and become an entrepreneur, what are your choices? With the main advantage (pro) and disadvantage (con), here is my recommended 'first action' list.

1   *Your job is made redundant*
    +PRO: Potentially you receive a lump sum
    –CON: It can be difficult to maintain a 'can-do' mindset
    ! FIRST ACTION: Use this unexpected career 'break' to
    think about and analyse what you really want

2   *Resign*
    +PRO: You need to make money, and fast
    –CON: Lack of income
    ! FIRST ACTION: Reflect first – consider your options
    below

3   *Start a company while working full-time*
    +PRO: You have two or more income streams
    –CON: You won't get much spare time and perhaps little or
    no sleep!
    ! FIRST ACTION: Look at online opportunities first, then
    to a student or house person who could run it for you

4   *Start a company while working part-time*
    +PRO: Two income streams and some sleep
    –CON: You would have to bring in more money, quicker
    than under 3
    ! FIRST ACTION: As 3, ask your company if you could go
    part-time, perhaps working 4 days a week

5   *Earn additional money while still working (without starting a
    company)*
    +PRO: More money at no risk
    –CON: Still takes time
    ! FIRST ACTION: Write a book (under a pseudonym?) or
    one of the thousands of other ideas out there

6   *Wait, and plan*
    +PRO: Planning maximizes chances of success
    –CON: Will you ever do it? And will someone else make
    money with your idea, first?
    ! FIRST ACTION: Have a clear personal plan in place

And running across all of these choices, is one piece of advice: if you have a family, and/or dependents, such a decision as this cannot be made by you and you alone. Share your thoughts with your partner, with your mum/dad, with your siblings, and listen to their advice. You don't have to take it on board, but you do have to listen and be responsible for the decision that you ultimately take. That said, it is far easier to start a company with total backing from your loved ones.

In helping you have these discussions, and progressing your thoughts on what and when you will do what you do, answer this series of questions, and be precise:

1   Do I really want to leave? The grass is not always greener. Consider a new direction in the company you are presently with.
2   If the answer to 1 is yes, then ask yourself what results/outcomes you want from leaving and working for yourself.
3   Prepare your business by getting as much done while you are still in your job. You have evenings and weekends and paid leave time off in which to do this.

Consider working part-time while setting things up. This will keep an income stream going, gain extra time to prepare what you are going to do, and each day compare which style of life you prefer – a dip-your-toes-in-the-water approach.

RESIGNING YOUR POSITION

Given that I have said that this is my biggest regret, why would I include it as an option?

Because if you do this, and your income stream dries up, you quite simply *have to* go and earn money. You have no choice. And when you absolutely have to do something in life, to survive, it is extraordinary what you can achieve.

Here are three approaches to helping you make your big decision about such a big change in your life.

1 *Gut feel:* yes, after all of that advice, and all of that reading, go with your gut feel – it rarely lets you down. Does this, deep down, really feel like 'you'?

2 *Pros and cons:* I have covered some in the box above, but what about your own? The age-old method of making two lists, one of positives, and one of negatives, is a useful tool.

3 *Act 'as-if':* Make the decision as if it is a real one, in your head. Then start thinking about all the things you are now going to do, how you are going to act, what new roles and responsibilities you are going to shoulder; imagine all the things that are affected by your decision to change and how you will cope with them all. See yourself and your loved ones, living out this new reality in your mind's eye. You will soon be thinking either 'Yes, this feels right' or 'No, I really don't want to do this'.

And last, but most certainly not least, beyond 'what' you would do and 'how', ask yourself 'why?'

Is it for personal freedom, to prove something to yourself, to make a difference in the world? There are thousands of reasons why people start companies and travel on this journey; there will only be one over-riding one for you.

So, why?

THE 'WHY' FACTOR

Entrepreneurship? Why take the risk?

In my experience, life does not have an A to Z. There is no diagram to show us the way and no index to look up our destination. However, there are plenty of collisions to veer us off course. In my case, it was the death of my husband in an accident in 2007. I was 29.

Change of any kind brings fear. When change is imposed on us, the fear is overwhelming. For me, being an entrepreneur allows me to write my own A to Z, while accepting that I will be obliged to change it in response to occurrences that haven't yet entered my realm of possibility.

An ability to view the inevitable diversions as opportunities is vital. Without them, I'm in for a scary ride.

I have ditched my manual and followed my intuition. I left my secure career to set up my own business coaching and consulting practice. I ignored my financial fears and invested in property to make homes for others.

I gained the confidence to finally write that book I've always wanted to, and to enter into travel and wildlife journalism, previously only an aspiration.

I'm not sure I qualify as a flourishing entrepreneur, or even a budding entrepreneur. Nevertheless, I have been planted in the ground, and I'm discovering which way my roots are going to stretch. Now, I am growing. And you know what? I deserve it, and so do you.

Jennifer Parratt, www.iglooconsulting.co.uk

YOUR THREE KEY ACTIONS

- Analyse what you really want from your working life and environment.
- Involve your family in your decision but don't let them make your decision for you.
- Think through and prepare to make the change.

The Journey of Hindsight continues at V Your Secrets – 13 How to Apply the Lessons from *The Secret* on page 157.

The Journey of Misadventure continues at I Your Self – 2 How to Get Ready for the (Bumpy) Ride Ahead on page 14.

HOW TO WELCOME DETRACTORS (YOU REALLY NEED THEM)

'Don't let the opinions of the average man sway you. Dream, and he thinks you're crazy. Succeed, and he thinks you're lucky. Acquire wealth, and he thinks you're greedy. Pay no attention. He simply doesn't understand.'

Robert G. Allen

SUMMARY

Just as you will have supporters, you will have detractors. If that is a problem for you, then please get over it. The day you accept it as a sign of your success is the day when you are going to sleep soundly that night.

On your Naked Millionaire journey, please know this: you *need* detractors.

Whether you are a speaker, an author or a business entrepreneur – you need people to pay attention to you and your work. If you can attract detractors, because of your message, then all the better! And if you can attract them because of who you are, then, wow.

OK, point made – now let's turn to you, and how you can get used to this idea, come to terms with some or indeed many people not agreeing with you and telling you and others about it, a lot faster than I did.

I made my 'in the moment' leap from loathing to loving detractors. I even used to reserve time on a Friday afternoon for phoning them, one by one, to try and turn their opinion around – imagine how tired that made me for the weekend, and what a waste of time it was! My transition was all thanks to a guy called Barry Dunlop (www.barrydunlop.com).

Barry is a shy, quiet, retiring sort of guy, keeps himself to himself, and has no real opinions about anything. Really? No, rather the opposite, and I thank everything for that.

It was Barry who asked me the same question I ask of others: 'What result do you want?' When I told him, he then asked: 'And does having detractors help you, or hinder you?'

And that was the moment I got it.

Not just logically, emotionally too – in my heart.

Don't be logical, and ignore detractors. Respect their rights to say what they want, love their existence, and then get on with what you are doing.

'Controversy is more interesting than agreement. Controversy fuels curiosity.'
James Cameron, film director

Because they can't stop you.

It is a self-fulfilling prophecy: you need detractors in order to be successful, and when you are successful (by your own definition) you will attract them. So don't go out of your way to avoid them, and don't be afraid of them.

In Naked Leader we now put our detractors right up there on our website. Not to have a go at them (that gives them more power), not to say they are wrong (they are perfectly entitled to express the opinions they believe in); rather to say – 'Here, look at this, there are different opinions out there, and here they are, now make up your own mind.'

Nothing anyone says has any meaning other than the meaning you choose to give it.

Just like when your teenager tells you that they 'hate you', you know they don't really mean it, so when a detractor says something about you, be strong enough to turn it around.

> Reggie: I couldn't help noticing when we first met, that you seemed happy.
>
> Sue: Yes indeed.
>
> Reggie: How do you do that?
>
> Sue: I don't know really. Someone once said to me, 'Sue, you're a bit simple, aren't you?' I took that as a compliment.
>
> Reggie: Even though it isn't one.
>
> Sue: Well, I think it is.
>
> Reggie: Well, it isn't.
>
> Sue: Well, I think it is.
>
> *Reggie Perrin*, written by Simon Nye and David Nobbs

'Lead me, follow me, or get out of my way'

Adopt those ten words, or your own variation, and you will avoid the pitfalls that detractors can use to trap you.

Because they may well have valid points about something you are doing, your company or anything else. And when you are considering their views – and these may be negative people, detractors, within your company – say to them:

'Lead me… Go on then, show me the way, take me forward, share with me what to do, help our company by telling us what we should be doing, not what we should not be doing. It is the easiest thing in the world to focus on what we could not be doing. What could we be doing instead?'

Or

'Follow me… OK, you have chosen not to lead me, or us. In that case I/ we invite you to follow us – trust me/us to take you forward.'

Or

'Get out of my way … Neither of the above? Fair enough. However, while you sit on the fence, I have a life and career and business to get on with, so please excuse me, and the best of luck to you and yours.'

The power of detractors was well illustrated in the media as I was writing this very chapter – I have no wish to help the party involved, and they would have a lot less power if they were just ignored.

The British National Party in the UK could not believe their good fortune. In October 2009 their leader, Nick Griffin, had been invited as a panellist onto the BBC's flagship political panel programme, *Question Time*.

This resulted in a mass breakout of anger against the BBC for giving a voice to someone with such extreme and repugnant views. Fair enough.

So, the detractors think: What shall we do to minimize the publicity?

Option A: Ignore it, let him go on and be a normal panellist – he will speak for about one-fifth of the programme time, and he is up against four other panellists who will be destroying his views, as well as a hostile audience.

Option B: Protest outside the BBC, fight with and injure the police, break into the BBC and be dragged out – creating virtually continuous news output for *Sky News* being shown all over the world (I now started receiving emails from around the world saying 'who is Nick Griffin and the BNP?'). And of course they went for Option B.

I am not saying they were 'right' or 'wrong'. I am merely repeating the facts of the day and evening, to show how detractors can help accelerate the very thing they are detracting from.

And, once the panel show gets started, what are the questions focused on? The postal strike then bringing Britain's postal system to a halt just nine weeks before Christmas? No. The continuing war in Iraq? No. The then desperate state of the world economy? No. That night they focused on just one topic – Nick Griffin – who spoke, and most crucially, was spoken about, for the vast majority of the programme. The following day the papers and news and country were full of it.

You couldn't buy publicity like that – and the BNP didn't have to.

Question Time with Nick Griffin was watched by the highest audience in the programme's 30-year history – over 8 million viewers, 3 times its normal audience, 10 times ITV1's audience at the same time.

Source: BARB – Broadcasters Audience Research Board

YOUR THREE KEY ACTIONS

- Expect and celebrate detractors. Never argue with them.
- Be yourself at all times.
- Always believe in what you do, or don't do it.

The Journey of Hindsight continues at III Your Business – 8 How to Unlock the Holy Grail of Fast Business Growth on page 104.

The Journey of Misadventure continues at I Your Self – 3 How to Form Key Relationships (People and money) on page 20.

'Success and failure are the same impostor.'

Rudyard Kipling

SUMMARY

Beware the 'impostor syndrome' – a fear of being not enough, or of being 'found out' as inadequate or a 'pretender'. Accept it as a sign of your success, or remove it by jumping to the end of this chapter and simply read on…

Within a short period of my coaching senior leaders, they will almost always share with me this fear, which is a variation of this conversation:

'David, I have a big presentation to make at head office tomorrow – parent company is flying in from abroad. It's the biggest meeting I will have ever attended.'

Then he stops. I use some questions that are known as 'clean questions' (see www.judyrees.co.uk for details).

I ask him the first 'clean question': 'What kind of meeting?'

He continues: 'Company performance, and it's going well; company perception, that's going well; delivery against key results for this time of year, that's fine.'

I remember the second 'clean question': 'Is there anything else about the meeting?'

And then he opens up and speaks for nearly three minutes, at an incredible speed – the words cannot come out fast enough. He is scared of one thing, more than anything else: of being 'found out'.

When he has finished I tell him like it is: 'Everyone gets really scared, sometimes.'

Does this apply to you?

If yes, great. This fear can in itself be a powerful driver to keep going, especially when you're up against the odds.

If no, you are one of the lucky few.

I call it the 'impostor syndrome'; it is so prevalent it has been referred to as the 'impostor phenomenon'.

THE SYMPTOMS

The impostor syndrome comes in a variety of guises. It generally feeds off a feeling that somehow you have achieved your success by accident, by good timing, by chance; that sooner or later, someone will come along and expose you for being the 'fraud' that you really are. You have fooled the world all around you each and every day, but you have not fooled yourself. You know that one day you will be found out, so you meekly accept your fate, and, almost relieved that you don't have to keep up this pretence any longer, you bow your head, apologize and go home.

Michelle Dewberry, winner of the second series of British television's *The Apprentice*, brilliantly calls this feeling one of being found out 'by the reality police'.

If it is a driver for successful people – is it really a pitfall?

You decide.

Does having these feelings of being inadequate, of not having deserved all that you have achieved – of being an 'impostor' – serve you, help you?

146

If so – if you have these feelings, and you are really enjoying yourself when you have them, then great!

All the CEOs and entrepreneurs I coach, to a man or a woman, would prefer to carry out their responsibilities, enjoy their role and feel comfortable in their position without the distraction of wondering when they will be 'found out'.

You might be the exception, either not having those feelings or embracing those feelings and finding them useful to achieve your goals – if so, there is no need to read on.

NOW, what if you could be driven to achieve your ambitions without these feelings of self-doubt?

RETURN TO YOURSELF

You did not have any feelings of being an impostor when you were born.

You know this is true; however, deep down, it is not enough to remove your deep-seated doubts.

When you were a child at a playground and your friend shouted to you, even though you were standing right next to him or her: 'The slide! The slide!' what did you say and do?

Did you say 'Yes, yes, beat you there!' or 'Hang on, what about Health and Safety?'

You know which.

You know, deep down. Sadly, those feelings of the self-assured, liberated and confident you are very deep, and buried by years of conditioning.

What I am going to share with you next will resurface your natural, inner strengths, confidence and talent. On first reading it may appear simplistic – that's because it is. It has to be – you have had complexity for most of your life, so more of it won't help.

Besides, whether it is 'simple' or 'complex' does not matter. What matters are the results for you...

Regain the confident you

How can you remove these years of layers of falsehoods, and unlock your deep-seated feelings of confidence (with just enough humility thrown in)?

Simple. Read this – it doesn't matter where you are. If you wish to listen instead, download it free at www.nakedleader.com.

Some people imagine going into a very relaxed, calm state, just by the way that they use their imagination.

While you are reading this and turning over the thoughts in your head, can you imagine being relaxed? Just for a second?

See in your mind's eye looking down what this looks like.

Listen for the quiet, calm and small noises of peaceful relaxation.

Feel the chair beneath you gently supporting your body.

Just pretend for a moment that you no longer have any feelings of being an impostor – those feelings that you had are being put to one side, just so we can make believe what it feels like not to have them.

One way to play this game is to replace these feelings and act as if you are feeling confident and happy, for no reason whatsoever. In fact, just by reading that sentence once again – one way to play this game is to act as if you are feeling confident and happy, for no reason whatsoever – and you thinking whatever you are thinking, it may well be that you are feeling just that little bit more relaxed than you were just now.

That's right.

Now, you might choose to allow in these feelings of peace and calm and slower breathing, or you might simply just go with the flow.

Whoever and wherever you are right now, just pretend for a few moments that you are very comfortable.

Now, what's it like when you recall an experience you once had, that made you feel very confident and self-assured? Remember that situation right now – be there, in your mind, right now.

See what you saw, hear what you heard, feel how you felt.

Very good.

It's as if your mind is taking you on a journey inside, to a very peaceful scene that you are reliving right now, like it is the most natural thing in the world.

I want you to experience these feelings for yourself, so you discover for yourself that you are indeed in total control.

Always.

You may notice these words are becoming slightly longer. It may be that your eyes are relaxing more as you read, or it may be that you are not just reading the words, you are reading the g a p s b e t w e e n   t h e   w o r d s

And that's fine.

As soon as you notice you are reading more slowly, and you are breathing slightly more slowly, you will realize that you and I are connected, as one.

Indeed, it is like these words have been written just for you.

From now, whenever you blink, as well as whenever you breathe, as well as every word you read, will rise in your awareness.

And every time you read this, you will find the feelings you have right now, of being very very centred, are doubled.

And again.

And again.

To the point where you perhaps realize the truth that is deep within.

Yes, you have been told you are this.

You may have been told that you are that.

And now for a simple fact.

You are.

You are, aren't you?

Who else can you be?

You can only, ever, be you.

The you that you have always been.

Sooner or later, perhaps now, perhaps next, you will realize this one fact about you.

You were born you.

You grew up as you.

And right now, once again, you are you.

Will you accept that, now, or will you accept that later?

How will you know when you are being you?

You will.

Because these words are and have been taken in deep into your subconscious mind.

Where your natural, unlocked talent is waiting.

That is not being big-headed.

That is not being small-headed.

It is just being you.

You are not forever striving to be the very best that you can be, or struggling to be more than what you have become. You are simply being the very best that you already are.

The best that you were on the day you were born, the best you always have been, the best that you always will be.

The very best, that you already are.

Consciously, these words are like a key, to unlock your conscious feelings, skills and personality.

As you read them with your conscious mind, they unlock the safe that is your subconscious.

And when a key unlocks a safe – that safe has to open, it has no choice.

Because you always have been you.

In all that is.

And all that was.

And all that will be.

And now, as you think about that idea, and you keep reading, it is just possible that you are remembering the real you.

It may seem like a long time ago, or it may feel it is just a moment ago, or it may be right now.

Time does not matter right now.

These feelings of relaxation can enter your inner self very fast, or they may take slightly longer.

Just as they will last as long as you want them to – indeed, they will.

A feeling you will remember.

Every day, in every moment, you can choose to remember these natural feelings.

Whenever you think of a special, unique word that is yours.

In your mind, think of a word right now.

Stop reading until you do – a word that has meanings for you that you can see, and hear, and feel.

Now, you have a special, unique and private word – that is yours and yours alone.

And whenever you say that word, silently to yourself, wherever you are, feelings of calm and relaxation and joy will come rushing through you like a warm radiator.

You need not even think about them, simply expect them, and look forward to them when you say that word just to yourself.

They will happen easily, effortlessly and automatically.

And it's a good thing for your adventure as a Naked Millionaire, as well as a good thing for your health, and in your relationships.

There's no need to say the word, until you choose to say it.

And when you do…

In a moment these words will stop, and the feelings you have right now, will keep going.

Consciously, and unconsciously.

In all that you do, wherever you are, each and every day – especially when you say your word.

And you can experience these feelings as often as you wish, as if you can have them forever right now.

I want to end with two little words, that, along with everything else you have read, will forever return you, to yourself – read the words, and hear their meaning, because I do sincerely mean them, directly for you, for reading this.

Thank you.

YOUR THREE KEY ACTIONS

- Realize that feeling like an impostor is a signal for success.
- Accept the feelings, as long as you accept them as the real you.
- Help other people realize it is OK to feel like that, and it's also OK to remove such feelings.

The Journey of Hindsight ends at V Your Secrets – 15 How to See What is Hidden in Plain Sight on page 177.

The Journey of Misadventure also ends at V Your Secrets – 15 How to See What is Hidden in Plain Sight on page 177.

YOUR SECRETS – SEE WHAT OTHERS DON'T

HOW TO APPLY THE LESSONS FROM *THE SECRET*

'It was really strange, the very moment I decided I was ready for a new challenge, I got the call from the head-hunter. Call it luck, chance or anything else you want – it happened!'
Barbara Simpson, on the call that made her director of organisational learning and talent development at Cancer Research UK; www.cancerresearchuk.org

SUMMARY

Best-selling book *The Secret* by Rhonda Byrne is based on the 'law of attraction' – what you focus on most, you attract into your life. So, think about what you want, never what you don't. This is very scientific, as it relates to the ways that our brains and minds are structured. It doesn't matter what you call it – 'positive thinking', 'synchronicity' or 'luck' – as long as you take action and do something about it.

In 2006 Rhonda Byrne wrote a book called *The Secret* with the central idea that whatever people focus on, they 'attract' into their lives.

Actually, let me pay her proper due deference. In 2006 Rhonda Byrne started a word-of-mouth phenomenon called *The Secret*. Not just a best-selling book, also a subsequent film and website community, with supporters and detractors in almost equal numbers.

The book simplified a historic idea – 'the law of attraction' – which can be summarized as: what you focus on, you draw closer to yourself. In essence, what you think about, you attract.

This so-called 'law' has attracted a fair amount of controversy in its time, mainly because it has often been misinterpreted to mean that all you have to do is to think about something, for that thing to come into your life. In my view, that is delusional. Focusing on something is important, but you have to do something as well. Positive thinking is not a strategy, just as negative thinking is not a strategy: you have to take action.

A second challenge to the 'law' relates to 'karma'. This suggests that if you have done bad things, then you will in some way be punished; for example, if you catch a cold then you have somehow attracted it into your life. This cannot be proved or disproved, so all I will say is that on your journey if you come across a very big challenge such as low cash in hand, that is more likely to do with low sales or people not paying you on time, than you dreaming about it.

The final challenge to *The Secret* is that there are many rude, unpleasant and thoroughly obnoxious people who are rich! Very few of these people are anything remotely close to being what I or they would call 'happy'. This book is about being wealthy and happy.

However, in principle, there is much to learn, take on board and apply from the 'law of attraction'. You are far more likely to take action and be persistent when you focus on what you want, rather than on what you don't want.

No matter how negative a situation seems, no matter how few choices you think you may have, and above all, no matter how others are reacting, *always* focus very clearly on what you want, what you want to happen as an outcome. Then, more ideas will come to you, on what to do. In addition, you will be in a more positive frame of mind, and have more energy to follow through and take action.

This works because of the way our minds are structured.

You have a conscious mind and a subconscious mind, sometimes called the unconscious mind (a term I avoid as 'unconscious' implies being out cold!).

Your conscious mind is the part of you that has conscious thoughts – ones that you are consciously aware of.

Your subconscious mind is the part of you that keeps your life going, by being aware of stuff, automatically, without you having to think (consciously).

When you are learning something new, like walking, it starts in the conscious mind – i.e. you consciously took your first steps, showing great bravery and persistence, until you could walk without falling over. Now, it is a subconscious – automatic – process. You can perform the actions of walking, without thinking.

The reverse – subconscious to conscious – happens in the following scenario. You are walking down the street, when you see someone on the other side who you do not want to meet, for whatever reason.

So you say to yourself, or if you are with someone else, you might say out loud to them: 'Walk normally.'

And immediately you or the two of you become like robots, walking anything but 'normally' and being consciously aware of each step you are taking and the (strange) movement of your arms.

For scores of years, psychologists have been fascinated by our conscious and subconscious minds, even holding debates on which part is more powerful! And then, a few years ago, research made a breakthrough.

It was discovered that when you believe something to be true with your conscious mind, the role of your subconscious mind is to make it true, and it starts to do so, straight away. Put another way: whenever you focus on something you want, your subconscious mind brings it closer.

That's the secret from *The Secret* and all of the other books on the law of attraction.

And it's not really a huge secret, is it?

HOW'S YOUR MEMORY?

Good? In that case, I expect you remember things; you have a 'good' memory.

Poor? In that case, I expect you don't remember things; you have a 'poor' memory.

If you have a 'poor' memory and wish to improve it, believe that you have a 'good' memory, and you will start remembering things.

If you have a 'poor' memory and you want your memory to deteriorate, believe that you have a 'poor' memory, and your memory abilities will disappear as if by magic.

And so, the thought, focus and belief are important – a launch pad to actually doing something.

With your memory, believing that you have a good memory will help, and you will then be more inclined to improve it further using specific memory techniques.

In your relationships, believing that you have a strong loving relationship with someone will help that relationship, and you will be more inclined to behave in a certain way.

On your journey, believing that your business will be a success, no matter what challenges you may be facing, will help, and you will then be more inclined to grow your business with positive actions.

And, if you take your belief further, to making a 'true decision' (you have decided on what you are going to achieve, and that you will settle for nothing less), you will notice things – events, phrases, books, etc. – that relate to the decision you have just made.

I have heard this referred to as 'life showing you the way'; in fact, it is you spotting the way for yourself.

Did those events, phrases, books, etc. that you are now noticing, for perhaps the first time, exist before? Of course they did. The only difference is that you didn't notice them.

We see the things that we look out for. That is why:

- Just when you believe a project can be turned around, the resources seem to appear.
- When you have decided that you can actually play the piano, or speak a new language, or anything, you learn the rest far quicker.
- The moment you decide that you will be a Naked Millionaire, you will start to see clues all around you as to what to do next to make it a reality.

When you focus on what you want, you are more likely to discover what you want ... when you believe that you are intelligent, you are more likely to see evidence that you are ... when you believe something to be true, you see the world in that way.

Especially so, because of what happens in your mind when you focus on what you do not want.

Whenever you focus on something you want, your subconscious mind brings it closer. And the opposite is also true: whenever you focus on something you do not want, your subconscious mind brings it closer.

And through a cruel twist of fate, it does it even faster than when you focus on something that you want.

Right now, wherever you are, do *not* think of a huge purple elephant with your mother sitting on top.

This is what happened.

Your conscious mind said to your subconscious mind – 'Do *not* think of a...' and your subconscious mind waited to be told what NOT to think of, so you added 'a huge purple elephant' to which your subconscious mind, not capable as it is, to think of something that does not exist, thinks of exactly that, straight away.

It's like when you say to your child: 'Don't touch the plate, it's hot.'

And they touch it straight away.

Like you did when you were a child.

When someone tells you not to think about something, you do – automatically.

You can't stop yourself.

Focusing on what you do not want reduces the number of ideas that come to you, to sort out an issue. In addition, you will be in a more negative frame of mind, and have less energy to follow through and take action.

Please, choose your thoughts with care, and choose your beliefs with great care, because they dictate your frame of mind to take action, or inaction.

Every day, focus on what you want, not what you don't want.

Surround yourself with positive people (that's people who think constructively, not destructively).

Surround yourself with negative, energy drainers, and you will get very tired, grow very cynical, and life will be a bitch.

Surround yourself with positive, energy givers, and you will get very energized, grow very positive, and life will be a choice.

'The law of attraction' is only half of the story; taking action is the other half.

There is nothing strange about this; it is logical and scientific. Science is the testing of hypotheses over and over, until they work every time – a 100% repeatable process.

When you touch one hand with another, they make a sound which we human beings have defined as a 'clap' – this happens wherever you are in the world. It has to – it is a scientific fact.

When you focus on a clear outcome – result – you believe that result is possible and that you have the abilities to achieve it and make it real – you will therefore notice more help, information and resources than you may have noticed before. You have to – it is a scientific fact.

Other ideas touched on in *The Secret* are:

Synchronicity

Swiss psychologist Carl Jung coined the word to describe what he called 'temporally coincident occurrences of acausal events'.

I'm not clever enough to understand that, so I will call these events 'meaningful coincidences'.

If you do not believe in synchronicity, you will never experience it. In other words, if you do not believe it is true, it will not be true for you – never.

Equally, if you do believe in synchronicity, you will experience it. In other words, if you believe it is true, it will be true for you – always.

- Have you ever been about to phone someone, and they call you first?
- What about that chance meeting with someone you haven't seen in years, in that unusual place?
- Another example would be watching a movie and seeing within the story of that film a metaphor for your own life

situation, or a phrase that you are seeking for a book title, or a lesson that will help you on the journey you are on.

These are all examples of synchronicity. It is quite normal, expected and predictable.

After all, you are part of the Universe (people on this planet), and the Universe is communicating with itself all the time (people communicate with people).

Serendipity

Serendipity is when an apparently innocuous or even unfortunate event turns out to be helpful in some way.

Penicillin, ice cream cones and the microwave are among hundreds of inventions that were discovered accidentally.

Isaac Newton's head may have hurt when that apple hit it – but thanks to that we now have an understanding of gravity.

Christopher Columbus was looking for a new way to India in 1492 and wound up landing in the Americas. Native Americans were therefore called Indians.

Luck

Are you a 'lucky' person?

If you answered yes, you joined with many successful entrepreneurs, millionaires and people who say that luck played a big part in their achievements.

If you answered no, you joined with many successful entrepreneurs, millionaires and people who say that luck played no part in their achievements.

Are you a 'lucky' person?

Taking this from a different angle, when someone else believes in you, it can accelerate your own beliefs in yourself.

I met Kay through our charity work with The Prince's Trust. Here, she talks about a brief aspect of her life.

Hello, my name's Kay Lima. I'm from Manchester, UK, and I come from a background where I've been in care and didn't really have much in life to start with. I was moving from foster home to foster home and getting into trouble and being a rebellious teenager.

At 17, I got on a Prince's Trust one-week course called 'Get Started with Music'. I learnt to play the drum kit, bass guitar and the keyboard. Since then, I have started promoting bands, solo artists and DJs in Manchester.

I'm 19 now, and I am in the process of setting up my own live music promotions company, eventually developing it into an events company.

This year has been a complete whirlwind and I feel lucky to be where I am. So if you need help with marketing events – I'm your woman!

To anyone out there who wants to start a business, whatever age – go for it! Because you only live once, it gives you a reason to live and if you work hard – you'll gain the rewards.

Remember my name,

Kay Lima

YOUR THREE KEY ACTIONS

- Think about what you want, not what you don't want.
- When you make a true decision, you are more likely to see resources that will help you.
- Choose your beliefs carefully; make sure they help you move towards your goals, not away from them.

The Journey of Hindsight continues at I Your Self – 2 How to Get Ready for the (Bumpy) Ride Ahead on page 14.

The Journey of Misadventure continues at VI Your Speaking – 18 How to Take Your Place as a World-Class Speaker on page 220.

HOW TO HELP OTHERS
(AND CHANGE THE WORLD FOR GOOD)

'In the short time that we all have, we would want to be remembered for the good that we have done.'

GBH – Alan Bleasdale

SUMMARY

You want to be rich, happy and fulfilled, that is fine, and the only way to achieve this is to help others, and 'put something back' in the form of money, expertise and your time. This includes helping other entrepreneurs, to the extent that an entrepreneurial economy really takes off or continues to flourish in your country.

You will never be rich (in money, in fulfilment, in life) without the help of others.

Being a Naked Millionaire is a balance between being yourself, being content and happy – and caring about others. By doing so, you accelerate your fulfilment, your riches and your rewards, which will come back to you in many ways, some anticipated, some not.

RECIPROCITY

There's a natural tendency, a powerful urge inside us all, called 'reciprocity', meaning that when you do something to help someone else, they will naturally want to help you and others. The idea spans all faiths and religions, and it is a very powerful force.

Reciprocity is the reason your wife or partner keeps a mental list of everyone you have entertained for dinner, and who has not invited you back ... a list that goes back many years!

Reciprocity is when you drop someone off your Christmas card list, and then, with a day to go, you receive a card from them.

There you were, thinking you were 'ready' for Christmas, and feeling relaxed, and now you are running around the house looking for any old card, writing the biggest lie going – 'Look forward to catching up in the New Year' – and racing to make the post in time.

If it is any consolation, thousands of others are doing exactly the same – reciprocity is everywhere, and within everyone.

Now let us take this reality of helping others, of reciprocity, to a wider, even more fulfilling level. The first line of this chapter read: *You will never be rich (in money, in fulfilment, in life) without the help of others.*

And I now add: *You will never be rich, unless others are rich as well.*

Yes, you read that right.

If others are not rich, how will you know who to emulate? How will you know who to turn to for help and advice? How will you know what your outcome will look like? How will you know that it is not an impossible dream, and can indeed be done? Others have to be rich to prove the point that I have already made – that there really is enough money in the world.

Remember, their success is not your failure.

Just as your success is not their failure.

> I was sitting in my aircraft seat in economy waiting to take off. An announcement came over the intercom saying 'We would like to apologize to our customers in first class this evening that the air conditioning is broken.' Much to my surprise, applause and cheering broke out from all around me. I was amazed; after all, how did the fact that the air conditioning in first class was not working, help them?
>
> Reproduced by permission of Sylvia Tidy-Harris

As human beings we often compare how we are doing against how well other people are doing. Actually, that is what I used to do; I now know that I was wrong. I now believe that as human beings we often compare how we are doing against how well *we think* other people are doing.

You may think someone else is more successful than you, doing better than you, living a better life than you. How do you know? Certainly money does not, by itself, buy you those things.

At this point I was going to list some famous people who admitted to being depressed or suicidal (the ones who have come out into the open and said so), plus some people whose money most certainly did not, or has not, brought them happiness. I can't make such a list, as it would fill a book in itself, and besides, you only have to read any celebrity magazine, watch the entertainment news or indeed pick up any newspaper to discover these stories for yourself.

I also won't make such a list because their failure is not your success.

Because the biggest driver, shared by all human beings, is to be valued, by other people and by ourselves: first, by helping yourself; and second, by helping others. Giving your time to charities, making money for your local hospice, or carrying that child's buggy down those stairs in the London Underground.

Who knows where it will end?

You may know about the 'butterfly effect' – how one small event on one side of the planet can have a huge impact on the other side. This is how it works.

You help an elderly lady who lives nearby to carry her shopping home from your local shop. You start enjoying the experience of helping others and so you decide to help others whenever you can. By doing this you feel good and 'helping out' becomes a part of who you are, and so you bring it into your journey to being an entrepreneur. Then you decide to join a network of online entrepreneurs. Within that community is someone who is having trouble growing his company, and so you decide to help him with some advice and he turns his company around as a result. Then he too helps another in this way and it spreads like wildfire until you have so many more entrepreneurs in your country that the economy becomes more constant and stable and your country becomes more successful and a major player on the world's economic stage.

SOCIAL ENTREPRENEURSHIP

This relatively new term 'social entrepreneur' has sprung up to mean people who dedicate their lives and business activities to helping others. Social entrepreneurs help find imaginative answers to their society's most serious problems, and they argue that it is enterprise, not governments, that will help the most needy in society.

Famous social entrepreneurs from history include:

- Dr Maria Montessori (Italy): developed the Montessori approach to early childhood education.
- Vinoba Bhave (India): founder of the Land Gift Movement, which redistributed more than 7,000,000 acres of land to aid India's 'untouchables' and landless.
- Florence Nightingale (UK): founder of modern nursing, she established the first school for nurses.
- Jean Monnet (France): responsible for the reconstruction of the French economy following World War II.
- John Muir (US): naturalist and conservationist who established the national park system.

This list, gleaned from various sources, is typical of the examples that are given as 'social entrepreneurs'.

I take issue with one major aspect of the most popular definition of being a social entrepreneur. Popular belief holds that one is *either* a social entrepreneur (caring, helping others through a specific project, generally not-for-profit), *or* one is a business entrepreneur (measuring performance purely in terms of profit and return).

I believe that thinking is flawed. You can, indeed you must, be both a successful business entrepreneur and a social entrepreneur if you are going to make the wider difference that you want to make.

That belief implies that being a business entrepreneur in its own right is somehow less 'worthy' than being a social entrepreneur. That belief takes us right back to the thinking behind the 'money is evil' belief. For the sake of moving on fast, let's go with its more common definition. A company has three bottom lines: financial performance, environmental impact and social impact. And that includes not-for-profit companies (charities, etc.), which make a profit and reinvest it in further expansion and good works.

You have three bottom lines: helping yourself, helping others and helping the environment. Helping yourself must come first, for without that you can't help others. It's like that oxygen mask announcement in a plane: 'Please secure your own mask, before assisting others.' Well, if you don't survive, those around you may have no chance at all! The same goes for money: if you don't have it, how can you assist others?

To be a Naked Millionaire, you must be both a business and a social entrepreneur. The moment you help someone through a big idea, or a number of small ideas, you are a social entrepreneur.

Helping to build an entrepreneurial country

This is about building the possibility, an agenda, a manifesto for a secure and vibrant economy based on entrepreneurs and small and medium business owners. In short, building an entrepreneurial economy.

Over the last 60 years, the global economy has alternated between boom and bust, between very good times and very hard times. We now conclude that these swings are a 'natural' part of economic cycles, to be expected and ridden out. Which makes it quite surprising that so very few people predicted the most recent global recession!

What have countries and their leaders failed to grasp from these cycles that are as predictable as a roller-coaster? *That the only way to permanent economic stability is through the success of small, medium and entrepreneurial companies.* Locally, in your village, town and city. Nationally, in your country – especially if you want to be one of the top-performing economies in the world. And internationally, around the world.

The government and public sector can't give us 'stability' – the public sector spends money it receives on taxes from the private sector. Large private companies will play a part in giving us stability, but only to the extent that they can be stable themselves. Overall, the biggest impact on economic success now and in the future lies with you – the small to medium entrepreneurial companies.

Consider:

- If every single small to medium company in the UK took on just one additional person as an employee, national unemployment would end overnight.
- China, India and the Middle East are on course to be the dominant economies of the 21st century, and are built on small and medium companies. Entrepreneurial teaching is at the heart of their universities.
- Smaller companies, and individual entrepreneurs, are generally more innovative (they have to have ideas and they have to make them happen).
- They have a greater flexibility to change, adapt and adopt new products and services to meet and exceed their customers' needs.

It is only through such an economy, built on by individuals and small teams, that the world will thrive. It is also the only long-term solution for so-called 'third world' countries – helping people in poorer countries to develop their skills, while taking ownership and responsibility for what they achieve.

Big business will of course play its part, and it must. Large companies across the world provide employment, careers and fulfilment, while moving money around in the economy. Pension funds also depend on their success.

For most big companies in developed economies, their leaders and people are honest and ethical, and they are regulated by well-established authorities. The public and charity sectors will play their part and play an important part in helping others, every single day.

Now it is time to place alongside these the entrepreneurial agenda. The 'entrepreneurial manifesto' if I may call it that, is very simple; and it applies in every country in the world:

Economic stability will only happen when we raise the profile, performance and positive influence of the small to medium enterprise and entrepreneur.

The only way to achieve sustainable growth, to have a stable and vibrant economy, is to value, support and encourage entrepreneurs, small and medium businesses, to be successful.

As I've highlighted above, during the last recession, if every single small company in the UK had recruited just one person each, unemployment would not only have disappeared completely, there would actually have been a deficit of employees!

But the UK government introduced some of the most far-reaching and complex employment laws ever seen. Further afield, employment restrictions in countries around the world are equally obtuse and counterproductive. I ask myself: 'Why would anyone employ anyone else?'

I am not advocating an absence of laws or rules or red tape, or arguing that the employment laws don't add value in some business sectors (e.g. solicitors, in order to interpret them). What I am saying is: please remember and recognize the entrepreneurial business sector when coming up with this stuff.

It is time to put entrepreneurs, small to medium businesses, at the very heart of our economy.

Not just because that is what you would expect me to suggest.

Neither because it will appeal to you because that is what you are, or soon will be.

Rather because it has to happen – as the only way to break the destructive cycles of boom and bust, while being the only way to help eradicate poverty in the world.

THE ENTREPRENEURIAL PROJECT

The outcome
To introduce, grow or stabilize an entrepreneurial culture in your country.

The results
- The future economy and stability of your country is secured.
- Your country is able to compete on the world stage in the new economy.
- Increased opportunities for the unemployed and for people wanting to change jobs; increased mobility between larger and smaller organizations.
- External business, academic and cultural investment is attracted into your region.

The how?
- Bring together all small and medium business owners, and entrepreneurs and all groups that advocate and represent this community, into a powerful network of networks online – run by themselves, for themselves.
- Secure the backing of the most influential leaders in your country – key politicians and parties, academics and business schools.
- Ensure that entrepreneurs help each other and use their success to transform the perception and status of being an entrepreneur within your country's culture.
- Take the lead with a strong and influential point of view on all issues.
- Help smaller companies to grow fast by focusing on innovation, export opportunities and the business (rather than red tape, form filling and other distractions).
- Connect companies and entrepreneurs in a network of networks that exchanges free information, help and advice. This will lead to a central knowledge base and a 'how-to' universe within your commercial community.
- Ensure that schools teach about and encourage 'success' and self-esteem in their curriculums, and encourage healthy competition at every level.

YOUR THREE KEY ACTIONS

- Be generous with your time and knowledge, and make helping others a regular 'habit' that reaps benefits for both helper and the helped.
- Help other entrepreneurs as you build your own business success; be a vibrant part of that entrepreneurial community network and really make a difference.
- Know that, as you do so, you are building a more stable economy for future generations.

Both Journeys – of Hindsight and Misadventure, conclude here.

The Journey of You continues, however, wherever and whenever you so choose.

HOW TO SEE WHAT IS HIDDEN IN PLAIN SIGHT

'Some people,' said Humpty Dumpty ... 'have no more sense than a baby.'
Lewis Carroll *– Alice through the Looking Glass*

SUMMARY

When you were a child, you had natural strengths that you still have. These include innocence (having a very open mind), passion (loving what you do), unconditional love (seeing the best in people), bravery and persistence (the ability to keep going), self-belief and just the wonder of life. Return to your true self, by awakening these natural gifts.

We can be so patronizing towards babies and children – pleasant, loving and so very patronizing.

Here's the 'secret' part that you may not know: every single 'natural' strength that you were born with, wherever it came from, you still have today.

And know this: people can start living from the age of a single second, with powerful ideas, dreams and contributions to make. And most fundamentally, these *wonders* of childhood, of youth, of being young, are still alive within us all, and we can, if we so choose, reignite them, anytime.

Have you ever met a cynical child?

Ms Honey: 'Matilda is quite bright; she can multiply large numbers in her head.' Ms Trunchbull: 'So can a calculator.' From Matilda, by Roald Dahl; screenplay by Nicholas Kazan & Robin Swicord

I invite you to consider the possibility that we adults have as much to learn from children, as we have to teach them. I also invite you to apply this thinking to being a successful businessperson, leader and entrepreneur. The possibility that people new to an organization have as much to offer as those with years of experience; the idea that the dreams and ambitions we had on the day our companies were formed are still within us and our people; and most fundamentally, that these *wonders* of starting something new, of being at the start, are still alive within each and every organization, and can be rekindled at any time. When we make that choice, we are being totally true to ourselves, and in many ways, we are thinking like a child.

> 'I do not think there is any thrill that can go through the human heart like that felt by the inventor as he sees some creation of the brain unfolding to success … at that very beginning, such emotions make us forget food, sleep, friends, love, everything.'
> Nikola Tesla, Croatian-born American inventor, 1856–1943

Innocence

Go with your son or daughter, with your niece or with your nephew, or with your neighbours and their children, to a playground. Open up your senses to what is happening before your very eyes. Soon, you will feel it – running through your body, with such zest, and power, it almost knocks you over. As you look around, at the smiling faces, the laughter and spirited play, you realize it has always been all around you, it's just that you hadn't noticed so often, in the last few years. As you watch and wonder at the life before you, you have a choice.

You can regret that such times have passed you by, that this was in a previous life, and sigh, quietly to yourself. Or you can decide that such times are still within you, that these feelings can again be rekindled, and rejoice, as loudly as you wish.

Now, in your mind, make a mental list of your dreams now remembered. When you get home, write them down.

And there is only one rule.

There must be at least one on the list that is impossible. Totally, ridiculously impossible.

Many, if not most, of the really great business ideas of the past have been described as 'impossible'.

> 'It's kind of fun to do the impossible.'
> Walt Disney

And when you have finished, stop and read what you have written, or look at what you have drawn. And as you do, just before that internal voice kicks in and starts to judge what you have written, and before you feel self-conscious at what you have done – please say this single word to yourself. *Innocence.*

> *'Work hard, play hard. Sure. These days it's more like work hard, go home and eat potato salad. Anything you ever find in an Innocent bottle will always be 100% natural and delicious – and if it isn't, get on the banana phone and make us beg for forgiveness.'*
> The Innocent Drinks Company;
> www.innocentdrinks.co.uk

Have an open mind – be open to new ideas and love your thoughts that, when you were younger, may have been called 'childish' or 'unrealistic'.

Like we adults can talk!

Compiled from e-mails, and at schools – worded from a teenager's viewpoint:

When my parents say 'Oh, you just want to have your cake and eat it too.' What good is a cake if you can't eat it? What, should I eat someone else's cake instead?

Or when they come in the lounge and say 'Are you not in bed yet?' No, I am here, in the lounge, watching TV.

When companies say something is 'new and improved', which is it? If it's new, then there has never been anything before it. If it's an improvement, then there must have been something before it.

Go ahead and be completely innocent, and dream bigger dreams. The very act of doing so, will reignite...

Passion

'My parents always encouraged me to be myself, and to have ambition. I formed my first company when I was twelve, and they thought that was a great idea. That is where my passion came from.'
> Andy Varley – Managing Director, Insanity Group;
> www.insanitygroup.com

You have a passion deep within you that is screaming to be unleashed. A mixture of conformity, learned behaviour and fear of ridicule (shyness) prevents us showing and sharing this passion with others.

It doesn't have to be like that...

Most organizations recruit on the basis of 'hard skills': measureable, technical, learnable skills. Invariably employees leave, or are made redundant, or fired, on the grounds of so-called 'softer' skills – their personality or attitude. How can we reverse this unusual situation?

Simple: reverse it. Next time you recruit someone into your organization, do so first and foremost on the basis of their *passion*. Ask different questions, invite new levels of opinion and openness, always asking yourself this single question: does this person have the attitude, the personality and the energy, to help us, and for us to help them, succeed?

Celebrate passion, help cultivate passion and live your own life with passion; and treat everyone that you meet, including yourself, with...

Unconditional love

You are not absolutely certain, just pretty sure that when you were younger, your drivers were different from now, perhaps...

More on love, and less on hate.

More on what could be, less on what might not be.

More on more, less on less.

How many organizations (people) do we know, that come from a place of love, each and everyday – where energy, and trust and kindness truly thrive? How many organizations (people) do we know, who truly love their customers, and 'kiss' them with an emotional experience, every day? Bring unconditional love into your team, in the shape of unconditional respect. Respect for each other's differences and beliefs.

The analogy of loving relationships can be applied to giving your customers and potential customers a truly emotional experience, as these three online services have proved. What can you do with your service and online presence to emulate these?

Stage 1 Courting
Letting your customers know that you are there and that you care about them, because you know what interests and excites them.

amazon.com do this by knowing what you like by what you browse and buy, and having it appear out of the corner of your eye, or to put in your own wish list. They also do this by having over 75% of the site updated by visitors and customers, as they list their own favourite books, etc.

Stage 2 Reaching out
Treating your customers well, calling when you are wanted, and caring about their needs.

First Direct (www.firstdirect.com) have a revolutionized banking service, and are consistently voted the 'most loved' company by their customers. When they started, many experts said telephone banking would never succeed, because it lacked the personal touch. Quite the reverse: with both telephone and online banking, customers say they receive a far better service, because everything at First Direct, everything, is geared around delighting their customers. Not retaining them, delighting them.

Stage 3 Building loyalty
By building loving (respectful) relationships with your customers, you are embarking on a long-term relationship which will be for life.

> eBay is possibly the most successful website, and business story, on earth, and it has achieved this for one reason above all others. Yes, it brings together buyers and sellers; yes it does this for absolutely anything; yes, it offers the opportunity to make and save money; and there is one additional unique selling proposition that makes a fond relationship so much deeper.
>
> *Reputation.* Our reputation (what people think and say about us) is very, very important to us. eBay know this, and it is this additional 'gold dust' that leads to the most fantastic service. This level of trust and authenticity in an online auction environment not always known for its integrity is quite an achievement. And most amazingly, buyers pay for their goods straight away, within seconds of their bid being successful. Beats a 28-day payment cycle anytime!

You are going to need that unconditional love, to show…

Bravery and persistence

These two complementary acts and beliefs run throughout this book and on your adventure.

David Festenstein has a business, Teleopen Ltd, which helps companies sell more over the phone. In 2008 he had a stroke which paralysed his right side and left him in hospital, unable to work and very worried about the future. He takes up the story: 'I made a remarkable recovery and then realized I had a great opportunity to help others in their recovery process. So I reframed the experience as a "stroke of luck". Entrepreneurs can learn a great deal when misfortune hits – I say this to you, please, please never ever give up.'

www.davidfestenstein.com

Keeping going when all around you have given up is one of the lost 'golden wonders' – some people are rejected so often as they grow up, they learn to expect it and fear it, and they do everything they can to avoid being rejected again by not doing anything at all.

Then we start to call it *risk*.

When we were younger, we didn't call it anything – we just got on with it.

That is why so many companies spend so much money on 'risk analysis', when in many cases they couldn't take a risk if their lives depended on it.

To take action requires remembering a time when you had...

Total self-belief

When we know that we have enough, that we are enough, and that no-one and nothing can ever take those away from us, we have self-belief. And more, we know that our self-esteem is actually enhanced by having people around us who think differently, because we know that while we have enough, we can always learn and discover more. Not in a big-headed or arrogant way, just in a way of quiet, silent certainty. After all, if you do not believe in yourself, who will ever believe in you?

When did you stop believing?

Ask yourself that question once again, as you remember...

The wonder of wonder itself

When I was a child, I loved going to Euston station in London. It was pure magic. All those people, and unbelievable trains, and those far-off destinations, and so many platforms. Now, I am no longer a child, I hate going to Euston station in London. It is pure hell. All those people, and unbelievable trains, and those far-off destinations, and so many platforms.

The question is this – has Euston changed, or have I?

The wonder of wonder itself – the wonder of wonder yourself.

Do you ever wonder?

Many 'grown-ups' spend so much time looking and learning, seeking and searching, for what could be, for answers and for ideas, they miss what is going on around them, here and now.

Right now, wherever you are – look around you at life. This moment you are now in, will never ever be repeated again in your life. Take it all in: the people, the weather, the nature all around you. Next time you listen to your favourite piece of music, do you really listen? Perhaps your mind drifts elsewhere – thinking about what you need to *do* next, instead of just deciding to *be* now. The way to do this is to do it: listen to the music, to the instruments, and how they come together. As other thoughts enter your head, acknowledge them, and let them go again.

Have you ever wondered?

- How innocent we all still are, and how curiosity can play a bigger part in our organizations, and our life?
- What passion you have within you right now, and the incredible results you will achieve when it is unleashed, each and every day (and you will still have plenty left over)?
- What it would be like to love, and to be loved, without condition? Do you 'love' your customers, your team?
- How persistent you really can be, when you awaken the child within you?
- The self-belief that is already within you, and the personal and professional power, and possibilities, it unleashes.

The extract below is from an editorial printed in the *New York Sun* in 1897.

We take pleasure in answering thus prominently the communication below, expressing at the same time our great gratification that its faithful author is numbered among the friends of The Sun:

Dear Editor –
I am 8 years old. Some of my little friends say there is no Santa
Claus. Papa says, 'If you see it in The Sun, it's so.' Please tell me
the truth, is there a Santa Claus?

Virginia O'Hanlon

Virginia, your little friends are wrong. They have been affected
by the skepticism of a skeptical age. They do not believe except that
which they see.

Yes, Virginia, there is a Santa Claus. He exists as certainly as
love and generosity and devotion exist, and you know that they
abound and give to your life its highest beauty and joy. Alas! how
dreary would be the world if there were no Santa Claus! It would
be as dreary as if there were no Virginias. There would be no
childlike faith then, no poetry, no romance to make tolerable this
existence. We should have no enjoyment, except in sense and sight.
The external light with which childhood fills the world would be
extinguished.

Not believe in Santa Claus! You might as well not believe in
fairies. You might get your papa to hire men to watch in all the
chimneys on Christmas Eve to catch Santa Claus, and even if you
did not see Santa Claus coming down, what would that prove?
Nobody sees Santa Claus, and that is no sign that there is no
Santa Claus.

The most real things in the world are those that neither children
nor men can see. Did you ever see fairies dancing on the lawn?
Of course not, and that's no proof that they are not there. Nobody
can conceive or imagine all the wonders there are unseen and
unseeable in the world.

You tear apart the baby's rattle and see what makes the noise
inside, and there is a veil covering the unseen world which not
the strongest man, nor even the united strength of all the strongest
men that ever lived could tear apart.

Only faith, poetry, love, romance, can push aside that curtain
and view and picture the supernal beauty and glory beyond. Is it

all real? Ah, Virginia, in all this world there is nothing else more real and abiding.

Santa Claus! Thank God! he lives and lives forever. A thousand years from now, Virginia, nay 10 times 10,000 years from now, he will continue to make glad the heart of childhood.

various sources

YOUR THREE KEY ACTIONS

- Learn from children that which you already know.
- Believe in the strengths that you had on the day you were born; have an open mind, love what you do, respect each other, be brave and persistent, have total self-belief and enjoy the here and now.
- Help others to do the same.

The Journey of Hindsight continues at II Your Brand – 4 How to Find Your Big Idea (It needn't be unique) on page 39.

The Journey of Misadventure continues at III Your Business – 7 How to Do the Essentials (and not be a busy fool) on page 85.

VI

YOUR SPEAKING – PRESENT AS A PROFESSIONAL SPEAKER

HOW TO PREPARE (NOT FOR THE TIMID)

'I'm sorry, I seem to have lost my notes – I have no idea who you are – sorry.'

**Introduction given to a first-time speaker
at a London event**

SUMMARY

Start your speaking career by addressing an audience at your local junior school, then follow up with a talk at a senior school where you are not known, and the final part of your preparation and training is to speak at a school where you are known by a child there. Have a clear message, be yourself and always answer the question they will be asking: 'Why should I care?'

The second biggest number of emails we receive, after 'I want to write a book,' is on the subject of 'I want to be a speaker.'

It always amazes me the number of people who 'want' what they already have! If you can speak, then you are indeed already a speaker.

Already, first stage done and dusted.

Seriously, what we mean here by 'speaking' is speaking to a group of people in public, and getting paid for it. I will tell you exactly what to do, to progress from where you are now, through the four stages of professional speaking.

0   Overcoming the fear.
1   Getting paid for speaking (you have to be good).
2   Earning a good living from speaking (you have to be great).
3   Getting paid a lot and becoming wealthy from speaking (you have to be world class).

STAGE ZERO – OVERCOMING THE FEAR

In 1984 Daniel Goleman wrote in the *New York Times* about a study on social anxiety, which researched what human beings feared the most. In response to a questionnaire, most people's number-one fear was walking into a room full of strangers, the second was speaking in public, and in third place came the fear of death!

In your speaking career, you will have to overcome the first two fears (not the third, with any luck; at least not for some time).

Walking into a room full of strangers – overcoming the fear

The fear is entirely in your mind – just reading that again, and remembering it, may reduce any fears you have. Remember most people in the room have the same fear. And also, accept that some people do not have this fear – so it is clearly a choice. Choose not to have that fear.

Put the fear to one side by just walking in to the room. You know you will have to do it at some stage, so do it, regardless of how you may be feeling. It helps to 'act as if' – act as if you are feeling confident even if you are not – stand taller (imagine an invisible string connecting the top of your head with the ceiling, pulling you taller), and behave as you would if you were feeling very confident. Make eye contact, smile and greet people warmly.

Walking into a room full of strangers – what to do

As you enter do a quick scan of the room, and look for someone standing on their own. Get a drink if available (so you have something to do with one hand), and walk up to the person who is on their own. Remember you are more confident than them, or they would have gone up to someone else already – no-one ever chooses to stand on their own in a group.

As you walk up, smile, say your name, shake their hand and then ask them something about themselves, e.g. 'What do you do?' or 'Where have you travelled in from today?' or 'What made you decide to come here today?' And, then do what so few of us actually do properly, *listen* to what they say and pay them total and absolute attention.

If you just spent five minutes with a person on their own and only asked them questions about themselves, you would have made one very good friend. If they ask about you, answer, and then turn the subject back to their favourite subject, themselves. Now, the getaway! You are networking here and cannot afford to spend all of your time with just one other person. Simply wait until he or she has finished a point, then say something like – 'Do excuse me, it's been lovely to chat with you', shake their hand and then walk meaningfully towards, this time, a group of three.

A group of three is your second choice when entering the room, if you can't see anyone on their own. Threes are better to join than twos, first because the two probably only know each other and probably want to be in the same position by the end of the evening! And second because of comfort zones. If you walk up to a two, they have to move slightly aside to make way for you. With a three, you can slip in between two people and it becomes a perfect four (watch how people stand as they shuffle to make a four). Wait until whoever is speaking has finished what they are saying, then say something like this:

'Hi, sorry to interrupt you,' (they will mutter, 'no no, not at all') 'my name is...' and then shake each person's hand – silently repeating each person's name three times to yourself as you shake their hand. Then say to whoever was speaking when you joined them, 'please, do carry on' and then *listen* as above. Leave threes as you leave a one, and then go to the next one, or three. And have your killer proposition (see Chapter 9 on page 116) ready, so that if you are asked what you do, you have it at the ready.

Or simply arrive early, and you will be in the room already when most people arrive – it will be your room. If you arrive first, then network with the organizers (and if you arrive before the organizers, go for a walk around the block!).

Overcoming the fear of speaking

Practise by speaking in front of your biggest critic – yourself – in front of a mirror.

Be prepared. Know what you are going to say – indeed, the best way to be spontaneous is to be very well prepared.

Just before you speak, ask yourself these questions: 'Is there really anywhere else I would rather be, right now?' and 'Am I as prepared as I can be?' When I ask myself these questions I know that, deep down, the answer to the first is always 'No,' and the second is 'Yes.' After all, it has taken a lot of time and very hard work to reach this situation.

So, when you ask yourself the same questions, be absolutely honest with yourself – you may have an initial feeling that you would prefer to be somewhere more comfortable, or familiar, but would you, really? If on the other hand you answer 'Yes, I would prefer to be somewhere else,' then go on and speak anyway (you have to, and you know you have to, and the action of doing so by itself will push your fears to the background). Then, next time you are back in more familiar and comfortable territory, ask yourself 'Would I prefer to be about to speak, right now, than doing what I am doing?'

And, if you think you need to be better prepared, again, it is too late, so speak anyway. Your goal is to make sure you cover what you have prepared – what you know – as best you can.

Put the fear to one side by just walking in to the room. You know you will have to at some stage – so just *do it*.

Meet as many of the people in the audience as you can, beforehand. Go around the room introducing yourself, or meet them at the door as they come in – shake hands with everyone, say your name and acknowledge theirs. You do not have to remember their names; you are at this stage looking for lively characters that you may involve in your session.

MOVING TO LEVEL 1 – BEING GOOD

If you ever want to get onto the professional (paid) speaking circuit, you have to earn your money. To achieve this level, you will first have to speak for free, and treat these free speeches as your apprenticeship. To fast-track your practice, speak to one of these three groups:

1 A school
2 A school
3 A school

Seriously, a school is far better than any other venue, for fast-track training! However, you might *also* (that's as well as a school) choose a community group, book reading club or local business networking event.

Do the school first, though!

The best school to start with is one where you are not known, where you do not know any of the children personally. Choose a smallish school – ideally a junior school. The sort of school where you will be fine, whatever your talk is like. Write to the school, say what you do and the message you can convey to young people. Say that you are keen to 'give something back', and if they are ever looking for a speaker 'for 15 minutes' at assembly to give you a call. And make sure you have any legal clearance that you might need to be working with young people.

Prepare what you are going to say, then follow the four fundamental rules of a good speaker:

1 Stick to your timeslot. *Never ever over-run.* (It is discourteous to your audience, to other speakers, and to your client. How can you advise anyone of anything if you can't even tell the time?)
2 Be yourself. Be brave enough to ad lib (the best way to be spontaneous is to be prepared; this will allow you enough thinking room to ad lib and look natural).

3   Make sure the content of your talk answers the three top questions all audiences ask themselves, in this order:
   • *'Why should I care?'* Make what you are saying relevant and meaningful to your audience – if needed, research in advance who they are. Also, mingle with them as they come in and ask them directly, 'What would you most like to get out of this session?'
   • *'Does this person really know what they are talking about?'* Establish your credentials and show your authority – this has been largely done in your introduction, and by being asked to speak in the first place. Add to this by demonstrating you know what you are talking about by being confident of your material. Avoid directly praising yourself – that has the reverse effect.
   • *'What's in it for me?'* Everyone wants a mix of being inspired, and useful practical ideas on what to do backed up by evidence or research, help to overcome a problem they have in themselves or their organization, and/or help them to move closer to achieving an opportunity. Again, plan in advance by asking the organizers of the conference the biggest issues being faced by the group you are speaking with.
4   Have one clear message you want to get across. Tell them the message at the start, then tell an amusing personal story relating to the message and conclude by what the message means for them.

If you have 15 minutes allocated, speak for 10 and then ask if anyone has any questions.

The reason I suggest that you start at schools is because children are very good at asking questions! They understand that when you ask a question, you really want an answer. When hands go up, point, with an open palm facing upwards, at a student and say 'Yes?' Answer their question briefly, looking straight at them at first, and then at the whole audience.

Simple.

You think?

Perhaps; more probably not. Because in over ten years of speaking at schools and with young people, I have never ever had an 'easy' question – the top three most asked questions are variations of these:

'Do you have a proper job?'

'How much do you earn?'

'Do you enjoy what you do?'

However, whatever the question, the same rule applies: whatever they ask, you must answer.

When questions are completed, end by thanking the school for inviting you along, then enjoy the applause. A few minutes after your talk (some children will want to speak with you), casually ask the person who is looking after you (a teacher or the headmaster) this exact question:

'What one thing could I do to improve my talk?'

And if they are polite and say, 'Nothing, it was great,' say 'If there was just one thing – please, to help me, what would it be?'

And when they tell you, say thank you.

After each talk, send a *handwritten* letter of thanks to the school head, with one piece of specific praise about what they do well at their school.

When you are ready, move on to school number two. Choose a school in your area, where you still do not know any of the children personally. Choose a big school. The sort of school where you may or may not be fine, depending on how good you are. Write to the school as before, this time saying you are an 'experienced school speaker', say what you do and the message you can convey to young people. Say that you are 'speaking at schools to give something back' in your work, and if they are ever looking for a speaker 'for 30 minutes' at assembly to give you a call.

At the start of your talk, calm your nerves by setting the tone and involving the audience if possible. My favourite opener is one where I quote some research that shows only one-third of people at a presentation will actually listen to anything that you say. Ask for a show of hands of who these are (most hands will go up). Say 'Thank you,' and 'If I was presenting to your parents, only a few of them would put up their hands.'

Some other 'ice-breaker' questions to ask…

Q: Who here loves going to school?

Add 'I used to hate school, until I left; then I really missed it.' (Teachers will love that.)

Q: Who here saw (name a really cool TV programme) the other day?

Add 'I'm not allowed to watch that in my house – I'm too old.'

Q: Who likes (name a band that is really popular)?

Say 'Some people say I look like (name the lead singer).'

The key from school two is to get you very comfortable with anything that might happen – always remember you are a VIP guest who is giving your time for free, so you will be treated with respect. At the end inject some fun and guarantee to raise the roof by saying 'I am very new to speaking, and have been very nervous today. Can I just ask that you help my confidence by giving me a huge American round of applause?' (If you are in America you will get one, anyway.) Or say they have been a great audience, and ask them to give themselves a deafening round of applause – then start clapping first.

After your talk, ask this question of a group of pupils as they leave:

'What one thing could I to improve my talk?'

They will tell you! And when they do, thank them.

After each talk, send a handwritten letter of thanks to the school head, with one piece of specific praise about how well you were treated when you were there.

Then, after school two, we move to the biggest test of all – school three.

Deep breath!

Choose a school where you know one or more of the children personally – your own, or nieces/nephews, or children of friends, or children from the road where you live.

This is the sort of school where you are going to have to work very hard. And you now have a new overriding goal, to impress the student(s) that you know, and who know you. This is important as a litmus test, and because they will be talking about you before and certainly after the event – and you do not want them to say you were 'bad' or, perhaps worse, 'OK.'

All the same rules as before, except this time, because you are known at the school, you can approach them more directly and just phone them.

A few additional tips.

Do not refer to your child or any children you know – that will be highly embarrassing for them; instead, make sure the person introducing you mentions who you know at the school. This adds extra fun or pressure – the boy or girl you know will feel special, then when you do well, they will be popular with their friends. And if you don't...

After your talk (not straight away), ask the child you know: 'What one thing could I to improve my talk?'

And when they tell you, say thank you.

If they don't tell you, then they won't be talking to you, because you screwed up big time. Accept it, learn from it, and get over it.

Write a handwritten letter of thanks to the school head, with one piece of specific praise about how open the pupils were, and that the main reason you selected that school was because of ... and name the child you know at the school.

Here's one for school three:

You: 'What question about school do your parents ask you, when you get home, that really annoys you?'

Pupils: 'What did we do at school today?'

You: 'And, be honest, what do you say in reply?'

Pupils: 'Nothing.'

You: 'Absolutely – now, would you like your parents never ever to ask you that question again?'

Pupils: 'Yes please.' (They are now in the palm of your hand.)

You: 'OK, this is what to do next time your mum or dad asks you what you did at school today – tell them.' (Pause)

You: 'Let me tell you a little secret: they don't wanna know – they are very busy people, and are just being polite – so, when you tell them, tell them everything – from the moment you arrived, to the moment you left – and make it last two hours.' (Pause for laughter)

You: 'I promise you, they will never ever ask you again.'

By the way, by doing this you will also be joining a not-so-secret campaign to improve after-school conversations between children and their parents.

In addition to schools, speak at local community groups, at your church, or at a business networking group. Speak about your business, your hobby, your passion – at this early stage, the subject matters less than the experience.

Also, joining group speaking networks will help you learn and share experiences. We have a free online group at www. nakedleader.com.

At schools you will face the unexpected. That is very useful for you, because it means that in years to come, when during a question-and-answer session someone takes the microphone and says to you 'This is a very nasty question, I am afraid' you can say to yourself – 'Nasty? I've spoken at schools, mate, to children. You think this is going to be nasty? Bring it on'.

That's it for practice!

When I spoke at my daughter Olivia's school for the first time, I was unsure and nervous. Yes, I had spoken at many schools, at bigger schools, but where I was not known, by anyone.

I asked her in advance: 'What could I do that you would like and that no-one has done at an assembly before?'

She paused, and then said; 'Bring sweets then, no-one has ever done that.'

So I did – I cleared it with the headmaster (who thought the idea very funny indeed) and on the day I had two large jars of sweets. Not enough for everyone, but hey, this is an assembly, these kids will have had breakfast, they probably won't want any.

I arrived at school very early, checked out the hall, got equipped with a lapel microphone and then my time came. I was talking about the internet, and I had 20 minutes, plus 10 minutes of questions:

I asked a question – 'Tell me, who owns the internet?'

One boy put up his hand to speak, and I picked up jar no. 1 and said to him, 'Yes, that's right, you do' and threw him a sweet.

Now, somehow, when we get older, we get a little bit slower. That can be my only conclusion from what happened next. Yes, my point was that the internet is owned by all of them, and I never in a million years expected them to get that point, all together, over 300 students, in a heartbeat.

One second, one hand and one sweet. The next second, over 300 hands, and only two jars! – about 150 sweets.

I was 150 pieces of confectionery short. And that was making the incorrect assumption that they would have just one each.

The teachers at the side looked like they wanted to intervene, but they didn't – perhaps concluding that I was a professional, who had done this sort of thing many times before. Wrong!

I considered leaving. I could make the fire exit in about four seconds, my car in a further twenty, and be home in half an hour. But I couldn't go home. My daughter was in the audience!

So out went the sweets. Imagine pure and total chaos. Now double it. Caramels were intercepted, children fought over Hazelnut Whirls, as Turkish Delights got trodden on! This was clearly their only meal of the day. And in the midst of it all I was shouting 'One each! – just one each!'

And then the sweets ran out. I said, 'Sorry, no more – please return to your seats.' And they did, some sitting on and squashing the occasional coffee cream, before eating them.

Then the headmaster walked onto the stage. He raised his hands and lowered them, and the hall fell completely silent. What power! He said, very simply and clearly, 'Please show your appreciation for David.'

And the whole room erupted with cheers, whoops and welcome applause. Yes, I had taken a risk, yes, I stayed behind to clear up the wrappers, and yes, I was Mr Cool at home.

The head called me the very next day, said thank you, and asked me to come back the following year. I said yes. He then added, 'Bring more sweets.'

The next year of course, I rode my luck too far, and caused my daughter so much embarrassment she didn't speak to me for weeks...

Expectations were running very high for my visit. My daughter was talking about it for days – for weeks – beforehand. The talk was in September, a full year after the previous one. I did indeed bring more sweets, and had worked out a great way of handing them out without repeating the same riot as the previous year.

I had also revamped my messages – in short, I was ready!

While being introduced, I couldn't help noticing the room was full to overflowing – including even more teachers.

The moment I was introduced, the sixth formers (who will tend to sit at the back at your school talk) started what must have been a pre-arranged chant: 'Sweets – Sweets – Sweets.'

I smiled and said, 'Later.'

They changed their chant to 'Now – Now – Now' and by this stage everyone had joined in. And so I said 'OK.'

And now to my amazing idea. Off stage I had hidden my secret weapon – a Santa hat and sack – with the sweets inside! How clever is that? I quickly put on the hat, and dragged the sack behind me.

You know how plays and films are said to have 'mixed reviews?' Well, I don't think it would be too harsh to say that walking on stage dressed as Father Christmas (well, wearing his hat), dragging his sack, in the middle of September, received mixed reviews.

The younger kids loved it – they cheered – mainly the younger ones. The older kids were equally delighted – they knew what was in the sack.

And Olivia absolutely hated it.

I glanced across to her and her friends – and they were all sitting, Olivia stony-faced, staring straight at me, with an expression that was very clear: 'You have embarrassed me, Dad, in front of my friends, and that means that when I get home tonight, you are dead.'

After the talk, distraught, she told me to promise that I would never talk at her school again. A promise I could not make, because I would not be able to keep it.

I was going back the following year, I was going back just once more, I was going back to make it right.

And so, next September, for the third and final time, I spoke to my daughter's school. I told her she did not need to be there.

'Don't worry, I won't be,' was her reply.

She was – in the same seat.

This time I handed out the sweets in advance, one each.

This time I left the dressing-up at home.

And this time, after getting much advice from many people, I turned the biggest lemon that ever grew on a lemon tree into the juiciest, most bubbly lemonade you could ever taste.

Not because I was being clever, more because I was desperate: I had a daughter to win over.

Introduction ... less excitement as the confectionery was already taken care of ... I took to the centre of the stage, and said:

'I would like to start by saying a huge thank you – you were the first school in the world where I shared the idea that you can literally achieve anything you want in your life – and entirely because of your reaction I have shared that message with schools all over the world.' (Huge cheer. Olivia sat still.)

'And, you were the first school in the world where I threw out sweets, and entirely because of your reaction I have shared sweets with schools all over the world.' (Huge cheer, Olivia sat still.)

'And, you were the first school in the world where I dressed up as Santa Claus, and entirely because of your reaction I have never ever done that again.' (Huge cheer. Olivia joined in.)

YOUR THREE KEY ACTIONS

- Get out to a networking event as soon as possible and practise your networking skills (walking into the room, circulating, listening).
- Write to a school asking to go and speak about something relevant to young people.
- Move up through senior schools, clubs and others – and above all, enjoy yourself!

The Journey of Hindsight continues at 2 Your Brand – 5 – How to Become an Obvious Expert (in a world full of them) on page 54.

The Journey of Misadventure continues at 17 – How to Move from Good to Great to Outstanding on page 207.

HOW TO MOVE FROM GOOD TO GREAT TO OUTSTANDING

'By the way, when you're telling these little stories, here's a good idea. Have a point. It makes it so much more interesting for the listener.'
Planes, Trains and Automobiles – by John Hughes

SUMMARY
To be a truly 'outstanding' speaker you must excel at building rapport with your audience. You must never use notes, you must tell captivating and relevant stories and you must listen to all feedback, and learn from it. Always, be yourself and speak from your heart – oh, and get a speaking agent.

The bottom line in being an outstanding speaker is this: *Be yourself, and speak from your heart.*

If you can't speak from the heart – don't speak at all.

GETTING YOUR FIRST PAID EVENT

There are several routes to achieving this, and they all come down to one simple question:

Why on earth would anyone pay good money to hear you speaking?

If you can answer that, your journey on the road to being a professional speaker is well under way.

Let's look again in more detail at that question.

Why on earth (what's in it for them?) would anyone (you don't really mind who) pay good money (the people are unlikely to be paying their own money, it will probably be their organization's but they still have to justify it) to hear you (as opposed to anyone else) speaking (as opposed to juggling, dancing or playing football)?

The answers will be variations on the following reasons:

1 They have heard that you are good at inspiring people (or frightening them) into taking action or improving their performance.
2 They believe that the message you offer is either unique, or you are the best person at delivering it.
3 They can afford you as opposed to someone else more expensive.

Let's apply these answers to what you can do to best position yourself for your audience.

First, get known – get into the media with a clear message, a controversial angle or a new approach to a problem. Do more free events for both experience and exposure. Never under-estimate the power of word-of-mouth recommendation in the speaking market.

Your message should either be unique (expect others to copy it eventually, although they can never copy how it is delivered) or, if it is not unique, you will need to be the most clear, concise and compelling at getting an existing message across.

Money is as important in speaking as it is in any and all other areas in life. How much you get paid equates to how much value your client thinks you can add to their organization. Part of that comes down to simple supply and demand: the more demand you are in the more you will get paid. Be flexible on how much you charge, depending on the level of demand for your services. Speaking fees vary just like any other commodity and service.

FROM 'GOOD' TO 'OUTSTANDING'

There are four key differences between those many speakers who are 'good' and those few speakers who are 'outstanding', other than being paid higher fees. You will know you are out-standing when:

- You build rapport with your audience, i.e. you win them over.
- You never use notes.
- You are a master storyteller.
- You listen to all feedback, and learn from it.

You build rapport with your audience

You are there for them, and for no-one else.

Who are they? What do they want to hear? Why should they care what you say?

Outstanding speakers answer these questions by having a crystal clear message, by how that message is delivered, and by ensuring they arrive at an event early, to network with their audience. This has the double advantage of building rapport and, more crucially, finding out what people want from you in terms of messages.

Greet people as they arrive, or go to the tables and greet at the table. Shake as many hands as you can. This is to build rapport individually and helps you locate two or three people who are the more outgoing or outspoken characters whom you can perhaps involve in your session.

Make eye contact during your talk. Mentally split the room into three groups: those to your left, to your right and in front. Spend an average of one-third of your time making eye contact with each group, switching between groups on every point you make. Never hold eye contact with any individual for more than two seconds.

Get off the stage, or better still never get on it in the first place. Walk around and among the audience. Again, treat everyone equally – if you walk up the left aisle four times, then walk up the right aisle four times as well; as with eye contact, give equal time, focus and attention to each area.

Yes, move around; however, for your really important points, stand still.

To achieve this mobility you ideally need a lapel microphone (not a hand-held microphone). Then you can move around and move your arms as much as you wish. Always check that it has new batteries in, and make the technical people your new best friends when you arrive at the event.

You never use notes

No, not even those annoying small cue cards, which take your eye contact away from the audience, occupy your hands, and take over your ability to raise passion with your ability to read passages.

And, for all you PowerPoint users out there, I can share with you how to use it to the best of its abilities: *don't*. You will probably already have seen the impact of a full day's PowerPoint presentation. It's called audience coma.

Does this sound familiar?

- The speaker has 30 minutes, and brings along 40 PowerPoint slides – and then proceeds to take 45 minutes anyway. Well, that is unless the chairman turns off their microphone.
- Presenters stand and read what everyone can already see, usually after they have promised 'I won't go through these one by one.'
- The slides are so full they are unreadable. Again, the presenter will often apologize for this with 'I'm sorry this is a very full slide.' Or worse still – 'I know you won't be able to read this at the back.'

PowerPoint is not some kind of crutch – it is a total distraction. The audience wants to hear from *you*.

As I write this, I can almost hear you shouting your question in advance: 'Come on, David, I have to use PowerPoint as I need to share some detailed information.'

OK, if you absolutely must...

- Keep them to a minimum – use no more than five slides per 30 minutes of speaking time.
- Each one should feature a picture or graphic as well as words.
- Never just repeat the words displayed on the slide – add to them, or clarify what you mean, in your own words.

All of this means that you are going to have to memorize the key points of your talk, and then deliver them with a freshness that sounds like you are being spontaneous.

How can you be spontaneous when you are so prepared?

How can you not be?

The best way to be spontaneous is to be prepared!

Ask any professional actor, who must deliver every line as if they have never said it before, night after night. Ask any professional comedian. Ask any outstanding speaker. When you see someone speak who you would put into that category, go and ask them what they do, that makes them so good (they won't mind!).

How to remember

Treat your message as a journey. Choose a familiar journey; say, a walk down your street from the end of the road, to the door of your house.

Your first point is to say it is great to be here (you will add specific reasons). Imagine you are standing at the end of your road, and the first thing you see is a giant cheese grater, grating out piles and piles of grated cheese – it is massive, perhaps 20 feet high, and cheese is pouring out all over the road and as it does so, the grater is shifting from side to side – you must to get round it to avoid getting grated!

That's it – you will now remember to say it is 'great' (grate) to be here.

You might now be thinking, 'Blimey, if I remember every point to that extent, I will use up all of my brain'. Don't worry; psychologists have concluded that we use anything from under 2% to a maximum of 10% of our brain capacity, and that includes remembering everything that you have ever experienced and learned in the whole of your life.

You get around the grater and you want to start with your message – let's say your message is a story about when you were at school. You are now at another familiar point on your road back to your house, when suddenly you are faced with a playground ahead – boys and girls in school uniforms playing football and hopscotch or whatever – they must be *big* and they must be *loud* and they must be *moving*.

Big, *loud* and *moving* – the key three things in memory: we remember the unusual, not the usual; we take an interest in the different, not the similar (this is why drivers slow down to look at accidents).

Map out all of the key points on your journey. Start by writing them down – in the exact order of your journey – and make them *big*, *loud* and *moving*.

Then go through them one by one until you can see, hear and feel the journey in your mind. Then go over and over and over and over and over and over and over and over and over and over it until it is learned off by heart, head and every other part of your body.

Now, you have a format to follow, without using notes, and here's the spontaneous bit – the journey is now one that you know so well, that you can return to it at any point should someone ask a question, or if you just want to add something that has popped into your head.

You are in total control.

Have a few points around your key message that you always include – for each event, choose a different journey.

Having no notes makes you look like more of an expert, makes you more spontaneous, and enables you to send through your notes for everyone after the event, the perfect way to establish ongoing contact.

After the session, about a week later, send through an email with the key points you made.

You are a master storyteller

We love stories – as human beings, we absolutely love them. They fire up our imagination, from when we are little children, to the day we die.

You should tell stories that your audience can relate to, and ones which contain some humour (ideally self-deprecating) which will help you win rapport as a direct result. This will increase the chances of getting your message across, and also of persuading your audience to remember what you said, to remember you, and what they did as a result, days, weeks, perhaps years afterwards.

As human beings, beings that behave/misbehave, we love to hear about the behaviour of others, through stories. So the truly outstanding speaker must master the art of storytelling.

Check out the film, *The Electric Horseman*, with Robert Redford and Jane Fonda. Robert's character has stolen a thoroughbred horse, because it was being abused for publicity's sake. Jane plays a reporter who has caught up with him to film his point of view. He is very nervous about being on film. Suddenly, before the camera is switched on (or so he thinks – it is actually filming) he launches into an amazing speech full of passion, energy and belief.

After he finishes, and the camera is switched 'on', he clams up and speaks in a very stilted, dry, careful way.

How do you become a master storyteller? Write stories (experiences) down as they occur or happen to you and keep them on file for future use. Backdate this to your earliest childhood memories and you will have no shortage of storytelling material.

And then practise, and practise again, and just when you think you are good enough – you practise again. At being expressive, at injecting inflection into your voice, and by sharing different versions of a story to see which works best with various audiences. If you have a young child, read them stories at night. If you don't, read them to a loved one or to yourself.

You listen to all feedback, and learn from it

Three types of feedback will be important to you when developing your speaking skills.

- *Your own.* You will have a gut feel of what went well and what did not. Every time you speak, write down one thing you did really well, and one thing you did not, and identify what you will do to improve it next time. By the way, when you make a bad presentation, something we all do, don't despair – learn from it, and improve. Offer to do another talk free of charge for the same client.
- *Your audience.* Watch their body language, in particular for their engagement with you – the most obvious signs are eye contact, and whether their bodies are turned towards you. Always ask afterwards, 'What one thing could I improve on?' One week after the event, call the person who booked you and ask them the same question.
- *Your agent* (see below). Ensure your agent calls the client and asks them for feedback (you often get more honest and direct feedback via a third party). Ask for copies of any feedback forms completed and read them all.

AGENTS

There is no shortage of speaking agents around – and you have two decisions to make:

I would recommend registering with a speaking agent, *if* you can find an agent who will represent you – there are three sure-fire ways of doing this:

- If a company asks for you to speak and will pay for you, the agent will find you. Trust me, they *will* find you, and you're suddenly on their books.
- If endorsements of your speaking are strong (i.e. from the free speaking you have been doing in your apprenticeship).
- If you have a published book, are well known as a celebrity or are widely known for having a specific, clear message.

Then you need to decide if you should offer your services to that agent on an exclusive basis or not.

I will offer the pros and cons on this one, and my recommendation – you choose.

Advantages:

- The agent will push you above other speakers they have.
- You will build more of an ongoing trusted relationship with your agent.
- You will have a partner in this strange and challenging world of the professional speaker.

Disadvantages:

- You may limit your bookings. If another agent wants you, they would have to go through your agent – by the time this number of people gets involved, the client's fee goes up, and yours probably goes down.
- Other agents may be offended (yes, this business is like everything else in life) and may resort to running you down

should the clients in question suggest they want you (they may do it very subtly, but do it they will).
- Your agency may go bust or get into financial trouble, and then you may not get paid, and you'll have to find another agent.

My recommendation

I had an exclusive agent for many years and it worked brilliantly. When the time came to change that, it was a joint decision so there was and is no fallout and we still work together to this day.

That said, I would recommend that you do not go exclusive – given your own hard work at promoting yourself and turning your name into a global brand, you will not need to do this.

The best route for you is the one that works; however, I would suggest on your website you go with the line used by excellent speaker Jim Lawless.

> *Please contact your favourite Speaker Bureau to book Jim.*
> Reproduced by permission of Jim Lawless

That is very clever – your favourite bureau – the one you trust.

A final piece of advice on speaking agents

Make sure you get paid. To help achieve this, have total transparency with your agent. Know the difference in monetary value between what your client is paying and what you are being paid. There is nothing more embarrassing than hearing from a client how much *you* have cost them, and hearing that it is double what you are getting paid.

Ask around from other speakers who they think is the best agent. The professional speaking business is a strange mix of competitive cooperation.

We are all in this together, even though we know that we all compete against each other.

And a word on who clients 'belong' to; this can be something of a 'grey area'.

Black and white: If you speak through an agent to a client, and that client wants you to speak again, they have to go through the agent. If you book them directly, you may make a bit more money in the short term, but you are being unethical and you will be found out.

Slightly grey: You speak through an agent to a group of people from different companies, and one of those companies wants you to speak again, for them. You have to decide what you do here – personally, I would still pass it through the agent who got you the booking. However, that client may decide several weeks or months later that they want you and come direct to you, and they may not even remember where they saw you speak.

Very grey: The client already has a direct relationship with you (it may be in a different department) – in this case, do what you think best.

General rule: Be as transparent, professional and fair with your agent as you expect them to be with you.

I end this chapter as it began.

The bottom line in being an outstanding speaker is this:

Be yourself, and speak from your heart.

If you can't speak from the heart – don't speak at all.

Enjoy your life, and career and earnings, as an outstanding speaker.

One absolute certainty in your life as a professional speaker is that you will face the unexpected. I have learned so much from watching other outstanding speakers:

At a conference in Malaga, Spain, for 500 plus people, all of the electrics failed, some lights exploded, much noise and panic, then silence, and darkness. The speaker before me simply shouted 'Is everyone OK?' 'Yes!' came the reply and so they carried on, while others who knew their job restored light and power, although the speaker did have to shout!

At The Comedy Store in London, for a business charity event, a speaker was walking amongst the audience when someone very close said, in a very loud voice, 'Excuse me, personal space.' So he sat on his knee, put his arm around his neck and gave him a kiss! Everyone laughed. You could only get away with this at such an event.

I was speaking at an event in Athens. The speaker before me was a real academic expert who was boring, and over-running! Everyone behind the scenes was trying to get him to stop. I was quietly enjoying myself (whatever anyone may tell you, all speakers secretly hope the presenter before them is not very good). A full hour over his time, he suddenly said 'I think I am getting the message that I should stop now.' With that, he walked to the front of the stage, and fell off! He was OK, and to this day, people in that company come up to me and say – 'I remember you, let me think, yes, didn't you follow that guy who fell off the stage?' This guy taught me the powerful lesson of always finishing on a high – although I do not recommend his strategy.

YOUR THREE KEY ACTIONS

- Practise rapport, memory, storytelling and taking on feedback.

- Then practise some more.
- Get an agent, and *get paid*.

The Journey of Hindsight continues at VII Your Book – 21 How to Turn It into a Bestseller (in reality and perception) on page 264.

The Journey of Misadventure continues at IV Your Warning! – 11 How to Welcome Detractors (You really need them) on page 139.

HOW TO TAKE YOUR PLACE AS A WORLD-CLASS SPEAKER

'Friends, Romans, countrymen, lend me your ears; I come to bury Caesar, not to praise him.'
Mark Antony's great oration, from *Julius Caesar* by William Shakespeare

SUMMARY

World-class speakers are interactive (best way – get off the stage) and spontaneous (best way – to be prepared) and they tell stories that are relevant to their audience. Oh yes, and they use a lot of threes...

Mark Antony's speech after the murder of his emperor is arguably one of the greatest speeches ever made, in fact or fiction. We will return to it, later.

You already build rapport with your audience, never use notes, you tell stories and listen to all feedback, and learn from it.

Now, to be world class, add that you will:

1 Be in demand across the world.
2 Take interaction to a totally new level.
3 Be obsessive in your preparations.
4 Treat everyone with courtesy, respect and warmth.

BE IN DEMAND ACROSS THE WORLD

To be world-class, you have to speak around the world. Blindingly obvious, perhaps, also the difference between 'opinion' (a good or outstanding speaker) and 'fact' (a proven, world-class speaker).

When addressing audiences in different parts of the world, bear the following in mind:

- Adapt your talk to the culture of your host country.
- Sincerely praise something specific about your host country and its culture.
- Learn a few words to say in the country's language, and say them first as part of your opener.
- To any international audience, speak more slowly and avoid colloquial metaphors or provincial references which may have worked in previous engagements but don't 'translate' well abroad. If you have translators, speak with them in advance and share the key points you will make.
- Ensure your agent covers the world, or has access to separate agents in different regions or countries, certainly in those where you are best known and where your speaking engagements take place.

TAKE INTERACTION TO A TOTALLY NEW LEVEL

You will make it clear, without having to say so, that this is their event, not yours.

- Identify, before you begin, at least three people in the room who you think will be up for some interaction, and some fun. Yes, that's the third time I have used this word, because it is so important. When you are speaking at an event, people will want you to be at the event, rather than going through the motions of just repeating what you do at all events. They want you to be fresh, to be alive and to show you care about them. You can only do that if you are enjoying yourself. So, enjoy yourself.
- Have the lights up in the room (not just on the stage).
- World-class speakers can shorten or lengthen their talk to allow for any circumstance – for example, someone in the audience suddenly sharing a deep personal feeling, thought or decision.
- Walk up to the front, after being introduced, from the back of the room, through the audience.

In addition, world-class speakers know that people make decisions to change their lives, or even their organizations, based on emotions. The best speakers in the world engage in emotion.

Ben Zander has the audience remember, and find peace with, someone they have lost from their lives, as he plays a piece of Chopin music.

Tony Robbins takes his audience on a journey to the point of their death, having not achieved everything they wanted to have achieved.

If you think of something that takes the emotion of your audience to the same or similar levels, you will join the very few elite speakers on this planet.

BE OBSESSIVE IN YOUR PREPARATIONS

Develop a repeatable process for all of your events. Have a checklist of what you need to do and take, and follow it religiously.

- In the pre-event briefings, listen to what your client wants and expects from you. Be in no doubt, repeat it back to them so you can be sure. And ask everything about the event, the audience, the room – and what outcome is wanted.
- Arrive early, at least 90 minutes before you are due to speak. Check how long it will take you to reach your venue. If it works out at 40 minutes by train or public transport, treble that time.
- Know everything about the room, before the audience arrives. Walk around to check the view from every angle and to plan where you will walk. Does the floor squeak? Where? Check acoustics with the microphone.
- If possible, for balance, don't have one flipchart behind you, have two; place yourself in exactly the middle of the room; check that every chair near the front is the same colour and style, etc.

TREAT EVERYONE WITH RESPECT, COURTESY AND WARMTH

- Your client, of course.

- If a company driver collects you at the airport, build rapport with him or her as if they are the most important person on this planet. By the end of the journey you will have them opening up about the company, about what they like or don't like, or at the very least you will have them opening up about themselves.
- The person assigned to look after you. Ask if you can do anything to help in any way – I have seen top global speakers helping put the chairs out. Ask delegates you meet in advance what they want from the event. By the end of the day you will know the names of the key people, their background, what they do in the organization and/or at the event. They could be very useful in getting repeat bookings.
- The technical people. Absolutely critical – they have the power to destroy your talk at the 'accidental' press of a button. You need to get on with these people.

You may choose to make some additional money by selling your products at the back of the room. Your sales will be as dependent as much on how you treated people as on how your session went.

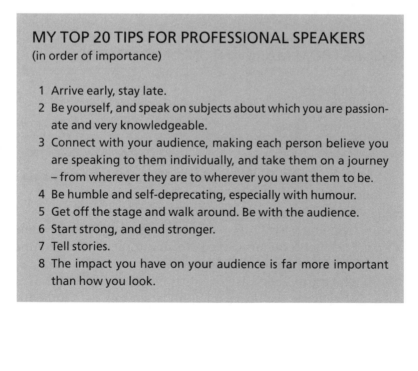

MY TOP 20 TIPS FOR PROFESSIONAL SPEAKERS
(in order of importance)

1 Arrive early, stay late.
2 Be yourself, and speak on subjects about which you are passionate and very knowledgeable.
3 Connect with your audience, making each person believe you are speaking to them individually, and take them on a journey – from wherever they are to wherever you want them to be.
4 Be humble and self-deprecating, especially with humour.
5 Get off the stage and walk around. Be with the audience.
6 Start strong, and end stronger.
7 Tell stories.
8 The impact you have on your audience is far more important than how you look.

9 No hype, jargon or mystery – make your talk accessible to all.

10 Be nice to people that you don't have to be nice to.

11 Involve your audience in your presentation early on.

12 Know your message well, and know your audience better.

13 Make it clear to your audience how they can apply what you have shared in their own lives.

14 Use three-part lists – (1) because it flows, (2) because it is the maximum anyone's brain can take and (3) because it feels complete.

15 Use contrasts – JFK: 'Ask not what your country can do for you, ask what you can do for your country.' Baroness Thatcher was at her most formidable when she famously told the 1980 Tory party conference: 'You turn if you want to, the lady's not for turning.'

16 Develop obsessive compulsive disorder (OCD) in your preparations.

17 Vary your voice.

18 Every seven seconds (maximum) change something.

19 Show your passion and emotion (don't act it).

20 Ask yourself how it is going – if you feel it is going well, then it is going well.

LESSONS FROM MARK ANTONY AND OTHERS

Mark Antony

'Friends, Romans, countrymen, lend me your ears; I come to bury Caesar, not to praise him.'

In just sixteen words, we see the three greatest speaking techniques used by world-class speakers:

- Opening with a three – 'Friends, Romans, countrymen.'
- Ending his opening line with an interaction that commands attention: 'Lend me your ears.'
- The use of a contrast that also gets the audience onto his side (they have just heard an anti-Caesar talk) – 'I come to bury Caesar, not to praise him.'

Check out the whole speech, watch it on film. Re-read the whole section on speaking and then read, listen to or watch Mark Antony. Then copy him!

American leaders

Jeremy Kourdi said the following at the launch of *The 100: Insights and Lessons from 100 of the Greatest Speakers and Speeches Ever Delivered*, a book he co-wrote with Simon Maier.

'Imagine if we combined a large number of American leaders and presidents, what might they say to you this evening:

'I have a dream, ladies and gentlemen. It's been a long time coming, but tonight, because of what I read on this day, at this defining moment, change has come. Our readers will have nothing to fear but fear itself; they will view every platform as a bully pulpit, and they will know not to make the pie higher.

'More than that, people will want to speak publicly – not because it's easy, but because it's hard. Because that goal will serve to organize and measure the best of our abilities and skills, because that challenge is one that we are willing to accept, one we are unwilling to postpone, and one which we intend to win. I have a dream today!

'So, ask not what this book can do for you – ask what you can do with the help of The 100.'

Barack Obama and Gordon Brown: a comparison

On Tuesday 4 November 2008, Barack Obama delivered his victory speech in Chicago.

See the speech on YouTube (search on Barack Obama on Election Night).

It was a masterclass in being a world-class speaker.

No, he didn't wander around the audience.

Yes, he did pretty much everything else.

He used the power of threes (many times):

> *'It's been a long time coming, but tonight, because of what we did on this day, in this election, at this defining moment, change has come to America,' he said to a long roar.*

'It's been a long time coming, but tonight, because of what we did

1   on this day,
2   in this election,
3   at this defining moment...'

Obama uses three points to illustrate what he could have said in one point, or indeed not at all.

Compare that to a possible alternative, one less than a three – a two.

Read both and decide for yourself which has bigger impact.

> *Three: 'It's been a long time coming, but tonight, because of what we did on this day, in this election, at this defining moment, change has come to America.'*

> *Two: 'It's been a long time coming, but tonight, because of what we did on this day, in this election, change has come to America.'*

Just as the two is underload, not quite enough, so one more, a four, is overload, as demonstrated by UK Prime Minister, Gordon Brown.

He chose these words to close his speech at the Labour Party conference in 2009 – his last conference speech before the General Election in 2010. And, on that most important occasion, in his most important speech, and at the most important point, the very end, he said:

'Because we are the Labour Party and our abiding duty is to stand. And fight. And win. And serve.'

1   To stand
2   And fight
3   And win
4   And serve.

Gordon, oh Gordon – why on earth did you have to add a fourth?

Let's travel back in time and change the ending for greater impact, using a three.

Clearly 'serve' is an important word, the most important. Let's remove it from the four at the end, and make it the 'abiding duty'.

Gordon's ending would have been:

'Because we are the Labour Party and our abiding duty is to serve. (Pause) And by doing so, we stand, and fight, and win.'

1   We stand
2   And fight
3   And win.

YOUR THREE KEY ACTIONS

- Be interactive (get off the stage) and spontaneous (be prepared).
- Tell stories that are relevant to the audience.
- Use the power of threes.

The Journey of Hindsight continues at III Your Business – 9 How to Know What to Sell (Sell it, deliver it and get paid) on page 116.

The Journey of Misadventure continues at II Your Brand – 5 How to Become an Obvious Expert (in a world full of them) on page 54.

YOUR BOOK –
WRITE A BESTSELLER

HOW TO BEGIN WRITING A BOOK (AND FINISH IT!)

'Well, of course, anyone can write a book.'
Caller to radio phone-in programme,
Auckland, New Zealand

SUMMARY

The moment you write your first word, you are a writer. Write about your big idea with passion, in the way that best suits you (dictate it, pen it, type it on your PC or PDA) at the time that best suits you. To overcome writer's block, just keep writing – it will come. And write what you enjoy writing.

The caller quoted above said in a sarcastic way: 'What's the big deal of having written a book and got it published?' I wanted my reply to be simply factual: 'Yes, indeed, anyone can.' And of course they can, including him, including you.

Of those people who want to write a book, most people don't. They think about it; they dream about it, they say things like: 'I've got a book in me.'

A book in you, how painful is that?

Anyone can write a book, but very few do. What about you: do you fancy writing a book, being a published author and making it a bestseller? You can. In this chapter I will share with you exactly what to do, and how to do it.

WHY WRITING A BOOK IS SO IMPORTANT

Writing a book can give you great credibility, and a published book will complement your speaking and expert career. Indeed, the publication of *The Naked Leader* gave me an almost disproportionate degree of credibility: 'He's written a book, and it's published, so he must know what he is talking about.'

So I continued to say much the same things I had said before the book was written; the difference was that now people listened to me, and believed me. Scary, humbling, and a great responsibility.

I remember how this book thing all started for me, like it was yesterday. I was having a coffee with René Carayol (www.carayol.com) in One Aldwych Hotel, London, in the summer of 2001.

René is the author of several books; his first was *Corporate Voodoo* in 2001. He was awarded an MBE in 2004 for outstanding service to the business community, is a great speaker, and has even trademarked his surname!

On that afternoon I asked René to give me one piece of advice, just one single piece of advice, over and above any other, that would help me on my own journey and adventure.

He looked me in the eyes and said: 'Write a book.'

And then he stopped talking!

Write a book.

I had that strange, momentary mixed feeling of fear and excitement that we all get when something is suggested that is way out of our comfort zone.

The fear. He didn't tell me what to write about, or how to write it, or where to get it published, or why anyone would possibly want to read what I wrote, and most of all he didn't tell me how to handle the complete abject feeling of failure when you have piles of books stacked high, unsold, unread.

The excitement. Wow – me – little me – a published author, could that be possible?

And then he broke his own silence: 'Would you like two other pieces of advice, as well?'

'Yes please,' I said, and gave him my complete and total attention. Perhaps he would be a little more, ah, detailed, this time. A bit more than three words please, René.

He looked at me square in the eyes and said 'Write a book.' OK, he was repeating his first piece of advice. Pause.

This was getting repetitive! Why did he keep saying exactly the same thing? Hopefully his last piece of advice would be a lot easier (more comfortable) than his first two.

'And' he said for a third time, 'Write a book.'

Then he sat back, smiled at me, took a sip of coffee, and fell quiet. The whole hotel around me – full of people going about their business – seemed to fall completely silent, and it was all very uneasy.

This man whom I admired so much, who had sat on the board of major global companies, had now given me nine words of his wisdom and advice – the same three words, repeated three times!

Nine little words that would change my life forever. For in that uncomfortable silence, I went from listening to reflecting to wondering to excitement to discomfort to confusion to absolute certainty and a true decision that I would actually do it.

Thank you, René.

And now I repeat those three pieces of advice to you:

1   Write a book.
2   Write a book.
3   Write a book.

As opposed to going around and thinking about it, and talking about it, and being jealous of others when they get their books published.

So get off your backside and put pen to paper, fingers to keyboard or mouth to recording device.

PLANNING WHAT TO WRITE ABOUT

That's easy, write about your big idea (see Chapter 4 on page 39).

Your book will have at its heart the idea, the belief, the cause that you stand for and that you will speak about at events.

Would you be surprised to find a book by Jeremy Clarkson on grass cuttings, or by Alan Titchmarsh on football, or Alan Hanson on cars?

Your book = your big idea, in words on pages.

There is no 'right' or 'wrong' way to go about writing. There are simply various ways and methods I can recommend, and you can use these or develop your own. Please feel welcome to share your experiences at www.nakedleader.com.

Method 1

Draw a vertical line down the middle of an A4 sheet of paper. On the left-hand side write down general headings, break your idea/subject/topic down into subsections and on the right-hand side list any specific thoughts, ideas and examples that emanate from that general heading.

Method 2

Dictate your thoughts as they come to you, into a machine
– whatever comes to mind, speak and record it. Take your
machine everywhere with you so you have it to hand whenever
you need it.

Method 3

Use a flipchart or A3 piece of paper and scribble/draw/write
your thoughts. Fill the blank space with as much material as
you can.

Method 4

Whatever works for you, i.e. whatever gets the ideas flowing,
the mind buzzing and the heart pounding. Maybe go to a special place (a library, some gardens) to get your inspiration.

The only way that works is the way that works for you.

As a result of this, you will now have a jumble of ideas/words/
thoughts in front of you, or recorded, or written on your bed-
room wall, or wherever.

Next, take time to *organize* your thoughts. To do this, there are
this time three methods I can recommend.

Mind-map

Mind maps, invented by Tony Buzan, are a diagrammatic representation of ideas and thoughts, which links them together
into a more organized and connected form. You can download
ready-to-fill-in online versions, or create your own from a

simple blank sheet of paper. Either way, they are hugely effective for people who like to think graphically (and that is most of us). If you are using paper do the following (source: www. mind-mapping.co.uk):

1 Start at the centre of a blank, landscape page, and draw or sketch ideally a colourful image to represent your subject.
2 Use words and pictures throughout your map. Wherever possible use single *key* words, printed along a line. Each word or picture sits on its own line.
3 The lines make the association between ideas as clear as possible. Make them flowing and organic, each line the same length as the word or image. Always ensure that lines connect to the end of the line at the previous level. Typically lines will be thicker at the centre and thinner further out.
4 Experiment with different ways of linking and connecting the various aspects of your map. Use highlighters, codes and arrows as necessary.
5 The structure that should develop will be a 'radiant hierarchy', with ideas radiating out from your central themes and main branches. This is a great way to see how different parts of your theme can link together and connect or feed off one another.

Post-it walls

Why should this fun way of organizing random input and data be reserved for training courses? Using any wall at home, write your central idea on a 'post-it' note and place it in the centre of the wall. Around it, place your subheadings/subcategories (the left-hand columns under Planning method 1) so that they form a large circle around your central idea. Now, write out third-level ideas and thoughts and place them in an even bigger circle, ensuring they are close to the second-level circle. This is a great way to see how your idea breaks down into a hierarchy of detail.

See where you go

Open a Word document and start writing – set out what you are about to do, and see where it takes you. Remember, you are writing about being about to write your book; you have not started writing your book yet. That comes next.

The above methods will help you take your big idea and start to link together ideas and the thoughts within and around it. Your aim from this is to start to plan the content and structure of your book, connect your ideas together, and most critically start to develop an 'angle' – a way of looking at your big idea which is unique to you.

Your book is *your book* – and that in itself makes it unique, because no-one else, other than you, can write a book, by you.

That may sound blindingly obvious; however, it is a fact missed by many writers, who seem to think they have to write in a specific style and special way.

You don't.

Well, you do – your own way.

So don't be frightened to really go for it. Write what you think – put your personality, the real you, into your writing. You can do this without upsetting other people or breaking libel laws. Be you and let the ideas flow.

In summary, your book will be about your big idea, with your own specific angle on it, and it will be as unique as you are.

HOW TO WRITE IT

There will be a moment when you move from going to write a

book, to actually writing a book. That is the big breakthrough that will set you on the path to completing your book.

And this is what to do, right now.

Go grab a pen – that is all you need for now, **go to the next page** of this book, which is left completely **blank**.

And write your first word – the first single word that will appear in the narrative of your book.

That's *not* the title of the book – it is *not* even the title of the first chapter – it is the first word that people will read of the book itself.

Go on, do it now.

No, stop thinking how crazy that sounds.

In this very moment, wherever you are, start to write your book. By choosing your first word. And writing it down.

And you have so many words to choose from – if you are writing your book in the English language, you have a big choice:

> 'The second edition of the Oxford English Dictionary contains full entries for 171,476 words in current use, and 47,156 obsolete words. To this total around 9,500 derivative words may be added.'
>
> www.askoxford.com

Don't worry if you don't know any derivative words (like most of us); that still leaves you plenty of choice with over 200,000 words.

Choose one.

And write it down – only read on after the once-blank page has been populated with something.

Well done.

And here's the rub – by writing down one single word, you may not have completed your book. You have, though, most certainly started it. You are no longer going to write a book, or thinking about writing a book – you are now, right now, actually writing it. You have gone from being a potential writer to being an actual writer. And simple though it may seem or sound, that is a *massive* psychological difference.

So, what's your first word?

When I wrote *The Naked Leader*, I gave it my all – literally, everything I knew about leadership and success – my brain dumped it all into a single book. And then I was asked to write a second book! I had absolutely no idea what to write – I felt I had written everything. And so I listened to my own advice, wrote the first word, well, actually two:

'Thank you.'

And once I had written those words, my book was being written. I was then a writer, once again. And now that you have written your first word or words, so are you. Let that fact – that feeling – run through you: you have done it, you have left behind all those people who say they will write a book, and never start.

Well done.

Now, *if you feel in the mood* (non-jargon word for *in the zone*), keep writing, all the way until you have completed your first sentence.

And, *if you don't feel in the mood* (non-jargon for *writer's block*), keep writing anyway, all the way until you have completed your first sentence.

No matter how you feel about what I am writing, or about anything right now – in fact, stop thinking and making judgements, and do what I tell you to do – because it *works*.

And when you have completed that first line, stand back and look at it. Not just because you have completed your book's first complete sentence, rather because you have now made your book your own.

Many books begin with 'Thank you' as their first two words. I completed the line to read:

'Thank you for reading this far.'

Quite possibly the best single sentence I have ever written (for a reason I will come to later on this adventure). Now the book was not just a book; it was my book. Write your first sentence – now.

Complete something very special. Something unique, something very personal, and something that you are literally inventing as you write.

The film *Flash of Genius* was based on the true story of inventor Robert Kearns' legal battle against the Ford Motor Company when they developed an intermittent windshield wiper based on ideas he had patented.

Ford's central argument was that all of the components to make the wiper had already been invented and therefore the wiper was not an original invention.

Kearns: I have here a book, by Charles Dickens, it's called *A Tale of Two Cities*. Have you ever read this book?

Witness: Yes, I read it in high school. It's a very good book.

Kearns: Yes, it is. I'd like to read you the first few words, if I may:

'It was the best of times, it was the worst of times, it was the age of wisdom, it was the age of foolishness.'

Let's start with the first word, 'It' – did Charles Dickens create that word?

Witness: No.

Kearns: What about 'was'?

Witness: No.

Kearns: 'the'

Witness: No.

Kearns: 'best'

Witness: No.

Kearns: 'of times' – look, I've got a dictionary here, I haven't checked but I would guess that every word that's in this book can be found in this dictionary.

Witness: I suspect that's probably true.

Kearns: OK, so then you agree that there is probably not a single new word in this book.

Witness: Well, I don't know, but that is probably true.

Kearns: All Charles Dickens did was arrange them into a new pattern, isn't that right?

Witness: Well, I admit I hadn't thought about it in that way.

Kearns: But Dickens did create something new, didn't he, by using words? The only tools that were available to him, just as almost all inventors in history have had to use the tools that were available to them. Telephones, space satellites, all of these were made from parts that already existed, correct, Professor?

Witness: Technically that's true, yes.

Source: *Flash of Genius* by Philip Railsback,
released by Universal Pictures

Having written your first line, and arranging the only tools that are available to you to write a book – words that already exist, words that you know about – you are an inventor.

And as you read that, and you think again about the first words that you have written, perhaps it makes you feel you have already achieved something very special. Great. That feeling won't last long, however. Pretty soon, you will ask yourself perhaps the ultimate question that all published writers ask themselves:

'How do I get this book finished?'

If your book is to be published by a book publisher (as opposed to by yourself) it will typically be between 65,000 and 85,000 words long. Now, as you look at that first word that you have written, or even your first line, the word *thousand* may well frighten you.

That is an important question to ask.

Because it is a better question than the alternative, asked by those who will have an unfinished book lying around at home, or lost forever in a computer file: *'Will I ever get this book finished?'* That question gives you the option of saying *'No.'*

Every writer will give you their own advice on completing your book; this advice is often conflicting.

Writer A	Writer B
'Write in the mornings.'	'Write in the evenings.'
'Plan your book carefully.'	'Don't plan – just write.'
'It's not what you write, it's the quality: better to write 100 great words than 1000 that you have to return to later.'	'It's not the quality, it's the volume – you can edit the quality in later.'

Then we have my favourite piece of advice:

'To write a book, start at the beginning, and then keep writing until you reach the end and then stop.'

I wish!

OK, here's my advice – and remember The Deal (there's only what works for you and what does not. I will tell you what to do and you will do what I tell you to, or you will do something else, until you discover what works, for you. With The Millionaire Deal, giving up is not an option.)

Best time to write	Whenever you want to – that's not the same as whenever you feel you have something to write. It is, quite literally, whenever you want to.
How to write	Sit down, or stand up, or dictate into a machine, whichever you choose to.
What to write	Whatever comes into your head. You can fit it all together later in separate sessions that are not writing sessions, they are planning/editing/organizing sessions.
What about style?	Write what comes into your head and heart and you will create your own style. As you write, you will know if what you are writing is any good (i.e. whether other people will enjoy reading it).
What about rules?	Just write! When we were younger we learned how not to write (never do this or that). A good starting point is to break every rule of writing you have ever learned.

And do you know what I love doing best? Beginning a sentence with 'and' – I was actually belted (that's right, corporal punishment) for starting a sentence with 'And' after being told never to do that.

Have your work professionally edited once you have finished. The investment you make in ensuring your book is professionally edited (every line, word and full stop) will repay itself many times over.

When you write, write, and set a ground rule for handling interruptions from other people. However, do not be over-strict with your family, especially children, if they do come and say hello – if you are, they will grow to hate your book as it is keeping you away from them. If you are so interrupted, take a break, scribbling down any unwritten thoughts just before you do.

Discipline

Our friend Wayne Moulds arrived at the house for a visit.

Me: 'Sorry, Wayne, would you mind putting the kettle on? I'm writing like mad here.'

Wayne: 'No, not at all – you on a roll?'

Me: 'No, not at all – I'm on a deadline.'

Writing can be a lonely business. Actually as I look at the clock in my library and it shows 4.54 am, I may have just written one of the biggest understatements of the century.

Distant deadlines, self-decided or imposed by others, can feel like they will never arrive; the pull of satellite TV and the urge to turn off that early alarm can all be overwhelming.

Develop a repeatable routine, perhaps with your own 'writing' music playlist that inspires you. I also carry my cats (Mozart and Sassafras) onto my desk when I start writing in the morning. They usually jump straight off; sometimes though, on special, magical mornings, one of them stays and keeps me company.

This is why completing a book belongs to the land of the very few, and not to the land of the many.

And yet anyone, *anyone*, can do it. If I can do it, anyone can. And that is not humility, it is a fact.

However, please read this personal paragraph and remember it. Every distraction, every reason for not writing, and every person who helpfully tells you to go and get a proper job or hobby will be but blades of grass compared to how you feel when you first hold your published book in your hands. It's like holding a newborn baby – because that is exactly what it is.

Lastly, as you write, if you enjoy the words you are writing, chances are that your reader will enjoy reading them.

Writing courses

There is no shortage of advertisements for writers 'colleges' or 'bureaux', and as with so many opinions on writing, the views on these are split.

My advice is to ask the advertiser for other writers who have been through the course, who have not yet succeeded in being published (they will only be advertising people who have achieved published status; you want to talk to someone who hasn't). If they say that everyone who enrols is successful, avoid them like the plague.

Remember, a writer who enrols on such a course may not succeed for many reasons, just like anyone who holds a pen or a keyboard may never start or complete a piece of written work, so it is not necessarily a reflection on the programme. You are asking to see how honest and open they are, behind the full-page adverts in the papers and magazines.

As with everything, there is only what works, and what does not. If they work for you, great. If not, find another way that does.

Overcoming writer's block

Just as marathon runners will tell you the best way to beat 'the wall' (i.e. exhaustion) is to keep on running, similarly the best way to overcome writer's block is to keep on writing.

Keep writing, anyway.

If you do get an 'attack' of such writer's block, and you feel you simply cannot write anymore, take a break, or change the way you are writing (switch from keyboard to pen), and above all be gentle with yourself.

One thing I know from every published writer is this: whenever and however they choose to write, they write. After a few minutes something automatic kicks in, when you can barely type the words as fast as they come to you.

THE IMPORTANT AND BORING BITS

- If you write or dictate into your PC or laptop, save what you are writing at regular intervals (you can set Microsoft Word to 'auto-save' mode).
- When you have completed your writing stint, email what you have written to yourself.
- Back up your PC/laptop every night.
- If you are handwriting your book, photocopy every page, every evening, in case you spill coffee on it!
- If you are as paranoid as I am, store it somewhere safe, away from your home (to be safe from both fire and burglary) – next door with a neighbour, perhaps.
- If you are dictating into a hand-held machine, check that it is recording before you start, and keep the tapes labelled and in a safe place.

All writing begins with reading. We learned how to write by learning how to read, and there are many sources you will draw on for inspiration and ideas. These are 20 of my favourite best-selling books – look through the titles, the key messages as I see them, and what I believe the author achieved. This list may help give you ideas on what read, what to write about, titles that sell, and what your core message/achievement/unique offering may be.

TWENTY BRILLIANT BOOKS

No.	Author	Key book	Key message	Achievement
1	Spencer Johnson	*Who Moved my Cheese?*	Change is down to each and every individual	Simplified how we are with regard to change
2	Steven Covey	*Seven Habits of Highly Effective People*	Leaders get into good patterns of behaviour	Principled leadership
3	James Redfield	*The Celestine Prophecy*	Synchronicity	Simplified synchronicity and sold over 10 m copies!
4	Colin Turner	*Shooting the Monkey*	Be yourself (it's the person you are best at being)	Eastern and Western thoughts combined
5	Charles Handy	*The Hungry Spirit*	People are pretty important!	Cultural change in a management context
6	Des Dearlove	*Business the Richard Branson Way*	A distillation of Branson's leadership	The ultimate in learning from the very best
7	Eckhart Tolle	*The Power of Now*	Live in the moment	Managed three books (so far) out of a single idea!
8	Mark Victor Hansen, Robert G. Allen	*The One Minute Millionaire*	Enlightenment in business just arrived	Written in two styles – as a business book and as story
9	Stephen Lundin	*Fish!*	Work can be fun!	Cultural change from the heart in story form
10	Rob Parsons	*The Heart of Success*	Leaders can have balance!	We are human beings at work as well

248

11	Warren Bennis	*Managing People is Like Herding Cats*	Leaders are made, not born	Leadership in reality
12	Dale Carnegie	*How to Win Friends and Influence People*	We are mirrors of our behaviour	How people are – similar and unique
13	Sun-Tzu	*The Art of War*	Opportunities multiply as they are seized	Action is all
14	Ken Blanchard	*The One Minute Manager*	Theories are great – now go do it!!	Management and leadership need not take ages
15	Wayne W. Dyer	*Manifest Your Destiny*	If we believe something to be true, it is	Popularized the idea of 'automatic destinies'
16	Nicolo Machiavelli	*The Prince*	Office politics happen – be the most powerful	Power is important to people
17	Deepak Chopra	*The Seven Spiritual Laws of Success*	We spend too much externally, not enough internally	Made the idea of inner selves clear
18	Edward de Bono	*The Use of Lateral Thinking*	Thinking outside the box	Started a phenomenon in thinking differently
19	Tony Buzan	*Use Your Head*	We think in pictures, and they improve connected thinking	Making mind-mapping a worldwide phenomenon
20	Adrian Webster	*Polar Bear Pirates and their Quest to Reach Fat City*	You will meet many different people on your journey to success	Combines cartoon fun with key messages for success

YOUR THREE KEY ACTIONS

- Write your first word, then sentence, then paragraph.
- Keep writing – write what you enjoy writing about.
- Celebrate along the way, and when you have finished, celebrate some more!

The Journey of Hindsight continues at VI Your Speaking – 16 How to Prepare (not for the timid) on page 191.

The Journey of Misadventure continues at III Your Business – 8 How to Unlock the Holy Grail of Fast Business Growth on page 104.

HOW TO HAVE IT PUBLISHED (WHILE STAYING SANE)

'American readers don't like animal stories.'
An American publisher rejecting George Orwell's
Animal Farm

SUMMARY

Write a one-page summary of your book and send it off to a publisher or agent. You will receive rejections and you will need to amend your submission. Send it off again – receive rejection, amend – send it off again – receive rejection, amend – send it off again – receive rejection – amend … And so on. At some stage in this process, you will receive an acceptance offer. No words can ever tell you how good that feels.

These authors are the stuff of publishing legend: JK Rowling, Stephen King, Jack Canfield – they all took ages to get their first books published. It seems as if it is a prerequisite for bestsellers to have taken a very long time to find a publisher to say 'Yes.' Their experiences are certainly important when it comes to two of the six things you are going to need: bravery and persistence.

FIVE KEY FACTORS IN GETTING YOUR BOOK PUBLISHED

1 A great title
2 A well-written book
3 A very strong single line that sells the book
4 Bravery
5 Persistence

A great title

Make it stand out, make it relevant and make it brilliant. You might even find the title is the last idea you come up with. Whenever you watch TV or films or listen to the radio, hear other people's conversations, listen out for stunning phrases that might apply to a description of your book.

When thinking about your book title, remember that most people buy and read it because they are looking for one or more of the following:

- Information (answers) on how to learn something, improve or change.
- Knowledge about something or someone they are new to, or need to know about, or are already familiar with.
- Success: how to be better, richer, healthier, promoted or more attractive – most self-improvement boils down to these.

Make sure your title clearly articulates how your book applies itself to one, or more, of these key drivers, and include a 'time promise' in the title if relevant, e.g. *Change Your Life in Seven Days* (Paul McKenna).

You will know when you come up with the perfect title because you will have an absolute, indescribable 'Eureka!' moment.

A well-written book

Ah yes, important, but not as important as the other four.

A very strong single line that sells the book

Sometimes called the '10-second sell' or, if you are American, 'the elevator pitch'. Craft a stunning one-liner that answers this three-part question: why would anyone buy this book, read it, and then recommend it to other people?

Bravery and persistence

Store these for later.

ROUTES TO MARKET

Your published book can these days take on one or more formats:

1   *A traditional physical hardback or paperback book* which arguably gives you the most credibility, and possibly the lowest royalties! But it also leads to higher coaching, consultancy or speaking fees. It is also, by far, the most difficult way to get your book published, because of the sheer volume of manuscripts received by publishers.

2   *An e-book* which will be downloadable onto your reader's computer. The big advantage of this is that you can publish your book yourself and keep more money for each book sold. The big disadvantage is it somehow doesn't feel so special or quite so credible as having the physical book in your hands, and it is hard work to do it yourself.

If you have a physical book that is also available from an online bookseller, readers may be able to pay and download it as a 'soft copy' onto a book reading device such as Amazon's Kindle or Apple's Ipad. These devices can hold more books than you will ever be able to read in your entire lifetime!

In terms of e-books alone (i.e the book has not been physically published) the fastest way to sell is to offer a download from your website.

For more information and examples, go to www.nakedleader. com

3   *'Vanity' publishing*

> *'A vanity press or vanity publisher is a publishing house that publishes books at the author's expense.'*
>
> Wikipedia

Whereas commercial publishers derive their profits from the number of your books that they sell, a vanity publisher derives profits from the amount of money that you pay them to publish it.

The publishing industry is full of different opinions and conflicting advice when it comes to vanity publishing, and it can all get very emotional. Not least because the term itself – coined by a publisher (Jonathan Clifford) – is rather derogatory.

Show me an author who claims not to be vain, and I will show you a liar.

My advice on vanity publishing is, don't dismiss it – having a book published and for sale at your events will give you credibility (not as much as if it is in shops or at the top of the Amazon charts, but some, and perhaps all that you need). Having a book that sells 'well' through your seminars (and in bulk quantities to companies) will help you attract a commercial publisher. Choose your vanity publisher carefully – join the book club at www.nakedleader.com for advice and ask around for opinions.

Print run numbers will depend on your budget and on the anticipated demand for your book. Print enough to last you 12–18 months, usually a minimum of 500 units up to 2000 or more, depending on your website, seminar and speaking activity.

Authors that self-published include:

A Time to Kill was first self-published by John Grisham. He sold his first work out of the trunk of his car.

After deciding to self-publish *The Beanie Baby Handbook*, Lee and Sue Fox sold three million copies in two years and made no. 2 on the *New York Times* bestseller list.

L. Ron Hubbard chose to self-publish *Dianetics*. Now, it has been in print more than 45 years, 20 million copies are in print, and it has been translated into 22 languages. The book started a movement and later a church.

Tom Peters chose to self-publish *In Search of Excellence*. He sold over 25,000 copies the first year. Then Warner picked it up and sold 10 million more.

The manuscript of *The Celestine Prophecy* by James Redfield made the rounds of the mainstream houses, and then he decided to self-publish. He sold over 100,000 copies out of the trunk of his Honda before Warner Books paid him $800,000. The no. 1 bestseller in 1996, it spent 165 weeks on the *New York Times* bestseller list. Over 5.5 million copies have been sold.

What Color Is Your Parachute? was self-published by clergyman Richard Nelson Bolles. Now it is in its 22nd edition, sold five million copies, and has spent 288 weeks on the *New York Times* bestseller list.

Getting your book into the bookshop

Most people would agree that getting your book published by a traditional publishing house is the most desirable way to reach the widest audience and see the largest return on investment. Most retailers only deal with publishers and wholesalers; the chances of getting your self-published title into a book store or available online are next to nothing without the backing of a professional publisher.

So, how do you get your book published in this way?

You can get a book agent or submit your book directly to a publisher.

Check out the writer's 'bible', *The Writers' and Artists' Yearbook*, for details of agents and publishers (see Appendix 2) and the kinds of book they specialize in. Send your potential agent or editor your book proposal, using the subheadings on the next page, or download this information from www.nakedleader.com. Make your submission no more than three pages in total.

YOUR NON-FICTION BOOK SUBMISSION

Overview

Title and 'killer line' that really sells your book and its benefits (it may go on to be your book's tag-line or subtitle). Write a brief description of the overall style, tone, scope and objectives of your book. Why are you writing this book and what makes it stand out as a great idea?

Market information

Who will be reading this book and why? Identify your primary and secondary audiences: who are you trying to reach? What's the market need for your book; what will people gain as a result of reading it? Also consider if there is anything specific happening in your area of expertise that makes your book particularly timely and relevant *right now*.

Content

Detail what you can about how this will shape up. Ideally you should have mapped out a structure and can show a sample 'table of contents'. Do you have any material you can send such as an introduction or sample first chapter? How long will your book be (number of pages/words) and when will the full, finished manuscript be available?

Competition

Why is your book different from the others already available in your area? List three titles that you see your book going head-to-head with, and include why yours offers something different or better. Be realistic and be honest.

About you

If *you* are a major selling point (i.e. if you are already an established name in your area), then include a biography earlier on in the proposal document, straight after the overview. Say as much as you can about who you are and why you are the best person to write this book. Include all contacts you have that will help promote and sell the book (articles you've written, blogs, podcasts or web communities you belong to and can influence, speaking engagements, corporate work, training). All of this contributes to your 'sales platform', your ability to highlight, promote and sell your book to the market. Include here lists of anyone influential or well known that you think you can get to endorse or write a review of your book. Also include any existing reviews you've had for workshops, online or other media or written work (send copies of clippings rather than originals).

SECURING AN AGENT OR APPROACHING A PUBLISHER DIRECTLY

The '7 step plan': (agent = agent or publisher)

1 Select an agent from *The Writers' and Artists' Yearbook*, send through your book proposal and call them to check that they have received it.
2 Wait.
3 Call the agent – they will not have read it as they are very busy. Wait some more.
4 Call agent – they will say they will read it tomorrow. Wait.
5 Call agent the next day – by now they will have read it because you will stand out with your persistence and you will be really pi**ing them off.
6 Call agent again. They will either say 'No thank you,' in which case get some feedback from them and return to Step 1, or they might say 'Let's meet,' in which case go to Step 7.
7 Celebrate!

You have not got a book deal yet, but you are about to get a face to face, which is fantastic.

The meeting

At your first meeting you will cover the book, the money and the next stages. However, do not treat this meeting as being all one-way. You might feel lucky to have a meeting with an agent or publisher, so you must convince them to take you on – but they must convince you as well. It will be a partnership.

Approach this as you would any other potential partnership. Be open and honest, go with your first impressions, ask good questions, and have great answers.

In advance of the meeting, research the publisher or agent online. In particular, find out which authors they publish or represent. If you are approaching a publisher directly, research publishers of books in their area, and find out the names of the relevant commissioning editors. Network with other published people in your area (this is useful in gaining a meeting in the first place, to seek an introduction or advice).

Other ideas include contributing to a publisher's blog or tweet about your book and offering to review a new book from that publisher's list.

For other ideas, join the writers circle at www.nakedleader.com.

At the meeting, be prepared to talk about your book in conversation, rather than repeating your one-page submission. Convince the person/people you are with that you are passionate about it – they will want to know that you will follow through and complete what you promise.

If and when the conversation goes well, proceed to money. With a publisher, this will split between advance and royalties; with an agent, it will be about percentage of advance and royalties. With your first book, you would not expect a large advance; indeed, you may not be offered any advance at all. Royalties are your percentage on each copy of your book sold and vary from, typically, 7.5% on paperbacks to up to 20% or more on hardbacks or specialist titles. Check if the publisher calculates your royalty on a percentage of the retail price or the net price. This can make quite a difference to your eventual share.

An agent will usually expect 15–20% of what they can negotiate for you.

If all parties are convinced by the conversation, then agree to go to the next stage – contracts. As with any type of contract law, consult a professional if you are not confident about negotiating a contract directly. If you have an agent, they of course will take this on and get you the best possible deal.

And throughout it all, and the process about to begin, expect, value and positively seek...

Feedback

- Show your book to your children as you write it, and ask for their honest feedback – they will give it!
- Contact a local reading circle or writers' club and ask them for their thoughts. Say that you will attend the meeting in person. They may be really nice to you to start with – so you need to expand on any negative comment. For example, 'I think it could have benefited from a slightly stronger opening paragraph' = in this person's opinion, you need to seriously improve that first paragraph, big time.
- Read your own book in a different way from how you are writing it – in other words, in a different location – go somewhere you would never go to write, and read it.
- Your partner or a loved one will provide a great balance between honest feedback and honest encouragement, unless the book has caused you not to be in the same room together for a year, in which case watch out!

'Flaming enthusiasm, backed up by horse sense and persistence, is the quality that most frequently makes for success.'

Dale Carnegie

And Dale should know! Born into poverty, after embarking on various careers, he then wrote a book which was rejected many times, but eventually published and is now one of the single biggest-selling books of any type and of all time. You might know it. It's called *How to Win Friends and Influence People*. Now, I encourage you to model (copy) every successful author on the planet – by showing *bravery and persistence* way beyond your comfort zone. Or perhaps in this instance that should be called your familiarity zone. Whichever, keep going until your friends are calling you 'crazy' and, most of all, until you succeed.

Every successful published author had to deal with rejection, so follow in the footsteps of those who succeeded...

- For every rejection letter you receive, say to yourself: 'How fantastic is this? I am following exactly in the path of every other successful published author.'

- Open some champagne and celebrate (do this for the first rejection only – otherwise you are going to end up very broke, and rather drunk).
- To confirm this, place the rejection letters in a prominent place – show them off to everyone who visits your home or office. Start by putting them on your notice board, and then when you have run out of room, put them elsewhere.
- On days when you don't have such self-belief, carry on anyway – this is too important to give up.
- Abandon your ego. You need those letters, you need the opinion of your close friends, you need every single piece of feedback you can get hold of – because you are going to take on board every piece of feedback you receive, and then decide if you will amend/change/improve your book, or not.

Stephen King (top-selling horror writer of all time)
'Sometimes all it takes is a little encouragement from someone who believes in you.'

Jonathan Livingston Seagull by Richard Bach
When he sent out the story, Bach received 18 rejection letters. Nobody thought a story about a seagull that flew not for survival but for the joy of flying itself would have an audience. Boy, were they wrong! Macmillan Publishers finally picked up *Jonathan Livingston Seagull* in 1972, and that year the book sold more than a million copies. A movie followed in 1973, with a soundtrack by Neil Diamond.

The Alchemist by Paulo Coelho
In his own words: 'My book *The Alchemist* was rejected after being published (which is much worse), as it sold only 900 copies in its first year. I started knocking doors, found another publisher who believed in this 'flop' and today I am in the *Guinness Book of World Records 2009* as the most translated living author (69 languages, 146 countries).'

Chicken Soup for the Soul by Jack Canfield and Mark Victor Hansen

Within a month of submitting the first manuscript to publishing houses, the creative team behind this multi-million dollar series got turned down 33 consecutive times. Publishers claimed that 'anthologies don't sell' and the book was 'too positive'. Total number of rejections? 140. Then, in 1993, the president of Health Communications took a chance on the collection of poems, stories and tidbits of encouragement. Today, the 65-title series has sold more than 80 million copies in 37 languages.

And to Think That I Saw it on Mulberry Street by Dr Seuss

Dr Seuss's first children's book was rejected by 27 publishers. The 28th publisher, Vanguard Press, sold six million copies of the book.

Zen and the Art of Motorcycle Maintenance by Robert Pirsig

Pirsig's manuscript attempts to understand the true meaning of life. By the time it was finally published in 1974, the book had been turned down 121 times. The editor who finally published *Zen and the Art of Motorcycle Maintenance* said of Pirsig's book, 'It forced me to decide what I was in publishing for.' Indeed, *Zen* has given millions of readers an accessible, enjoyable book for seeking insight into their own lives.

Star Wars

The movie *Star Wars* was rejected by every movie studio in Hollywood before 20th-Century Fox finally produced it. It went on to be one of the largest-grossing movies in film history.

Thanks to *Chicken Soup for the Writer's Soul*
by Jack Canfield and Mark Hansen

YOUR THREE KEY ACTIONS

- Publish without a publisher if you want to – you may make more money.
- Persist – take on feedback and refine your proposal in the light of it.
- Believe – abandon your ego.

The Journey of Hindsight continues at IV Your Warning! – 11 How to Welcome Detractors (You really need them) on page 139.

The Journey of Misadventure continues at 21 – How to Turn It into a Bestseller (in reality and perception) on page 264.

'It has been obvious for years that Richard Dawkins had a fat book on religion in him, but who would have thought him capable of writing one this bad? Incurious, dogmatic, rambling and self-contradictory, it has none of the style or verve of his earlier works.'

Prospect Magazine (October 2006) review of *The God Delusion* by Richard Dawkins, which went on to sell over two million copies

SUMMARY

Your book must identify with its readers and address their issues at a profound level (as if it is written just for them). As with your other activities, your book will attract detractors as well as followers. With the right combination of good content, good publishing, good marketing and reviews, get ready for it to become a bestseller.

You have written your book. Well done – that makes you one of the few, not one of the many.

Your book is published. Well done – that makes you one of the very few.

If you have come this far, you just have to go that little bit further. You have demonstrated amazing patience, focus, commitment, ownership and persistence. Now it is time to reap the rewards from your hard work, and make your book a bestseller.

Imagine that first moment when you see, touch and smell your new book, when you receive it from your publishers. This one is different because this book is yours – you hold it close.

What an achievement.

Over the next few days and weeks, you will hear people saying very nice things about your newly published book. You may read very positive reviews, and people will tell you that your book has changed their lives.

Ah, how sweet!

Over the next few days and weeks, you will hopefully also overhear people saying very nasty things about your newly published book. You may read very negative reviews, and people will tell you that your book was not worth the paper it was written on.

Oh, how sour!

Not so – you need people to be making both positive and negative comments about your book, if it is to be talked about and become a bestseller. Good news travels fast, bad news travels faster. Average news doesn't get off the ground.

The first published review of *The Naked Leader*, by Carol Kennedy in *The Director* magazine, included such putdowns as:

> *'This is why you shouldn't bother with books by non-leaders purporting to tell you how to be one. It's one of those pseudo-inspirational works … This is the sort of gung-ho conference stuff on which middle managers may get a momentary high. It's not a book for serious business readers.'*

I was later asked on the radio for my opinion on Carol's latest book; I said 'Take it or leave it.'

'The only thing worse than being talked about is not being talked about.'
Oscar Wilde

Most authors agree that even 'bad news is good news', except perhaps Salmon Rushdie, for whom it all went a bit too far. Quite a large group of people thought his book was blasphemous and they sentenced him to death. You probably don't want that. Mind you, it didn't hurt his book sales.

In fact, the worst thing, by far, is for your book to be ignored.

WHAT IS A 'BESTSELLER'?

That may sound like a silly question.

It's not. In the publishing world, never has such a term as 'bestseller' been so misunderstood, misinterpreted and misused.

A 'bestseller' can be *actual sales*, or *perceived sales* or *both*.

Book sales are either sold through the *trade* (in shops), *online*, *directly* (from the publishers) or through *corporate sales* – books bought directly from a publisher or author for an event, or for employees, or a customised edition of the book published just for that company.

The most accurate figures on trade sales can be obtained through BookScan, owned by the Nielsen Company. BookScan compiles point-of-sale data for book sales from a range of more than 20,000 stores around the world and from online retailers including Amazon. However, it does not include sales from all retailers or many independent bookshops. And it does not account for sales made to companies directly by a publisher or author.

So, BookScan sales are critical, but they are not everything – having a 'bestseller' changed with the arrival of Amazon, which turned the book market upside down. Now just 16 years old in the year 2010, Amazon is not just the largest online retailer in America (by far), it is also an author's dream. Monitoring one's book on the Amazon sales rankings has become the addiction of just about every writer out there (whether we admit it or not) and, unlike many addictions, this one is free.

Access any book on your local Amazon site and page down until you come to a heading on the left called 'product details'. Just below the star rating for average customer reviews is the Amazon sales rank number.

This is the popularity contest that your book will enter. Every time a copy of a book is sold, that book gets one vote in the competition, and unlike BookScan, which monitors total sales of books, Amazon ranks books according to how well they are selling online at Amazon relative to other books. So, in this instance, your book will be a 'bestseller' not on the basis of reaching a certain sales volume, but rather as long as it is selling more than other books, over a short period of time. In addition, Amazon ranks books according to specialist categories, e.g. business and investing, professional and technical, etc.

Boost sales of your book by getting your good reviews up on the Amazon site, and by linking to other best-selling books in your area. Make sure that the 'About the author' feature on Amazon is populated and get a video of yourself uploaded. Your publisher may be able to help you with a lot of this.

Finally, pre-order the book on Amazon, and encourage your friends, colleagues, mum to do so too – a few orders pre-publication can make a big difference to the ranking of the book.

TOP TEN FACTORS IN CREATING A BESTSELLER

10 The title

Make it special. Make it different. Make it the sort of title of a book you would want to buy.

9 You sincerely care about enhancing the lives of others

This will come across in your writing and in what people say about you and your writing. Put helping other people first, and be sincere in that, and it will assist everything you do, including book sales. Project that principle and passion in all that you say and do.

8   You know what the reader wants, their reason for reading

This is where being an *obvious expert* matters. Your book must be written as if it was written personally for each person reading it. You achieve that by ensuring your book appeals both to people's logic and to their emotions, with straightforward, practical ideas that the reader can put into effect straight away, in their own lives.

7   The subject must be of interest to or in demand by enough people

What books are in demand? Check out the Amazon bestseller lists: what is selling? What are people talking about on Facebook or Twitter? What films are coming out soon? Hit a trend wave just before the wave reaches its peak and see your book sales peak too.

6   Get your book reviewed

Draw up a joint plan with your publisher, that will see your book sent to any and every publication that might review your book. Put all reviews on your website and on Amazon. Your local papers are always looking for books to review. Send review copies to key magazines, journals and newspapers yourself with a covering letter. You are often better at selling the key points of your book than the PR department of a publishing house that has hundreds of books a day to deal with.

5   Be available for book signings and personal appearances

Again, with your publisher, approach bookshops and offer to do a book signing, coupled with a short talk about your book. Go for it – don't hide in the corner; advertise the event, approach people in the shop and, if you only have two people at your signing, treat them as the two most important people on the planet!

Be good on the radio and you will get on TV. Tweet, blog and let your supporters and detractors do the rest.

4   A viral word-of-mouth and word-of-web campaign

Do not expect your publisher to drive your campaign; they will have limited resources and many other books. Indeed, the irony here is that they are more likely to promote your book after it has started to look like a bestseller! It is up to you to take ownership of making it one.

So, be available to promote your book at every turn, to mention it at every event and in every interview or workshop you give or article that you write. Host the image of your book jacket on the front page of your website with a link to buy it from Amazon or other preferred retailer. Have it printed on one side of your business card.

3   The tipping point

This is the title of a book by Malcolm Gladwell that has become an everyday phrase. A tipping point is the moment at which something becomes so widely known that it enters the everyday conversation of many people. Once the 'word-of' campaigns kicks in, your book will 'tip', and it will become the 'in' thing to read. This is the stage when your book will be talked about by many people who won't even see it, let alone read it. That doesn't matter, because they are talking about it.

Consider employing a publicity agent. They can get you into other media like TV and film. It will cost a few thousand pounds, and you have to balance that with the reach they will provide (ensure they say what they will do), the time it will save you and the energy you could invest elsewhere.

2   Your book must be relevant to what is happening now

An effective way of making this happen is to keep up-to-date with current affairs generally and specifically in your sector; if something gets air time that pertains to your book, jump on it.

The relevance does not have to be for your whole book; it could just relate to a part of it. I once did five back-to-back radio regional phone-ins on five different topics, and drew out five different angles of my book. You can do the same – you can do it better.

1   *Your book is either* loved *or* hated *by someone you personally know*

On the day *The Naked Leader* was published, a leading academic wrote to all of his thousands of students, describing it as 'the single most dangerous book ever written' and adding 'Do not buy this book'. Many of them bought the book within a few seconds of receiving the email!

YOUR THREE KEY ACTIONS

- Have a full-on PR and marketing campaign around a simple and controversial idea.
- 'Bestseller' in perception is as strong as in 'reality'.
- Persist; many bestsellers take years to take off.

The Journey of Hindsight continues at 6 Your Speaking – 18 How to Take Your Place as a World-Class Speaker on page 220.

The Journey of Misadventure continues at II Your Brand – 4 How to Find Your Big Idea (It needn't be unique) on page 39.

SUMMARY

To become a *millionaire*, you need authenticity (the ability to *genuinely be yourself*), *bravery*, *generosity*, *perseverance*, the ability to *build trusted relationships*, *skills* and *products* around a core idea that *others will pay for*; you need a *business* with a *clear exit plan*, you need to *get paid*, and to make a *profit*. Along the way, this might involve *writing a book*, designing an *interactive website*, becoming a *world-class speaker*, *attracting detractors*, and being open to *life showing you the way*.

1 Be yourself – the very best that you already are, with the skills that you already have. Ask yourself: is there anyone else on this planet who has achieved what you want to achieve? Is this person from a poorer background than you, or with fewer resources at their disposal? If the answer is 'yes' then you can achieve the same, or more. Believing otherwise is an excuse. No more excuses; you do not have time for them and they will cause you to fail before you have even started.

2 Make a true decision that should it be necessary, you will put your whole being 'above the parapet'. Be ready for the consequences of high-profile living with all its supporters and detractors. Detractors only have a go at people who do something, to justify to themselves that it is okay to do nothing – and you need them, to achieve what you want to achieve.

3 Come up with a big idea. Make it something you know a lot about, and sound like you know a lot about it. It can be new and unique, or an existing idea, adapted, enhanced or simplified, as long as you do not steal someone else's intellectual property. Above all, it must be something that people will *pay money for*.

4 Build trusted, lasting relationships and always deliver what you say you will. In addition, be nice to people you don't have to be nice to – receptionists, cleaners, taxi drivers, etc. The way you treat such people shows your true character.

5 Put in place the four cornerstones you need: a business (with an exit plan); an interactive website with presence on social networks; products or services that make you money while you sleep; and a book or talk on your idea.

6 Get on the speaking circuit by speaking first at schools. You can also include local associations, groups and clubs, but make sure you include schools – they are the best training a speaker can ever have. Register with an agent or agents, and start building a reputation for great delivery, performance and results based on what you say and how you say it.

7 Get endorsements from influential people in your field. Collect them as you go and keep a contacts book or database.

8 Delight your customers – they are the reason your business exists.

9 Be generous to others – help them on their own journeys. Adopt a charity and put something back into your community. Help your country to encourage more people to be entrepreneurs.

10 Every day, have fun and don't take it all too seriously.

CASE STUDY: THE NAKED OFFICE

'If people knew what shit DT talked, they wouldn't go around
with their dicks hanging out'
A fan on the Woking FC unofficial fans forum –
www.cardsboard.co.uk

I remember the moment as if I was reliving it right now.

Sarah from Shine Television said that they were going to do a broadcast pilot (pilot for a series, which will be broadcast, no matter how it turns out) for television station, Virgin One, and they would like to audition me for it. Would I be interested?

This sounded exciting.

The idea was that I would go in and help a small company – yet to be selected – who were going through business difficulties, and they would film me coaching and advising and working with them through those difficulties. OK so far, I thought.

'And to show that they have been turned around and that they are now working as a team, on the last day of the week, the Friday...'

Ah, I thought, here is the exciting part. Don't tell me – I get them to jump out of a plane together, or to perform an air–sea rescue, or get lost in the Lake District...

No, I was wrong on all counts, as Sarah concluded her sentence: '...they will all come in to work, naked'.

At first I thought she had said something else – she must have done. When I realized what she had said, I was so thrown that I just blurted out, 'OK, that sounds fine'. She said they would call to make the arrangements, and the call ended.

No way. You must be kidding. And so I did it.

The programme had the highest viewing records for Virgin One when it aired in 2009, and *The Naked Office* was shortlisted for a prestigious Royal Television Society award.

Throughout the whole process, I was focused on one overriding outcome: that the company I was working with, onebestway, would benefit from this, as a business.

So, did it work?

Over to Mike Owen, Managing Director of onebestway, in his own words, unedited…

ONEBESTWAY

Where we were before

onebestway, a creative agency, was born in June 2000. There followed five years of steady growth, three years of rapid growth, one year of devastating downsizing and one further year of careful rebuilding.

The Naked Office experience happened in the first quarter of the rebuild year, year ten, and informed so much of what I did and decisions that I made.

I craved simplicity, speed and a purer self-awareness. For years I had considered myself, and was considered by many, to be very successful. An innovator, driven and 'a winner'.

And I often felt like a fraud. I felt like a cheap copy of 'the real people', just days away from being found out. My next move in business was rarely my own move. It was an imitation of something that someone else was doing. It took a kind of skill to choose the right people to emulate, and surely there was more to it than this?

If business or indeed life really is simply about taking a look at existing paths and choosing which one to follow, then all one can ever do is be as good as today's best. One can never better than anyone has ever been.

Unless you are brave enough to establish a new path, of course.

onebestway was good. And I really knew onebestway and I knew it was a flawed, imperfect, troubled beastie. I was unsure whether we were ready to start establishing new paths and whether the circumstances were right. I was unsure whether bravery was really stupidity, taking a team that was far from perfect on a brand-new and uncertain journey.

We did it anyway.

Where we are now

onebestway for the first time in almost ten years knows what it is. We have a clear market position, we understand what makes us different and better, we know what we are good at and we do it every day.

We are clever people with clever ideas and we are confident in our approach. We are clever marketing people with international award-winning design fulfilment capabilities too.

It's funny how in life you sometimes wait for 'permission' or 'just the right set of circumstances' to do or say things when really you know all along what you should and could be doing.

When answers come easy it can be off-putting. Surely big questions are only answered with painful, lengthy exploration?

Not so. Pause, think, get excited, believe in it then do it. Properly.

What we did to get from one to the other

onebestway knows what it is and how it is better because we understand the environment in which we exist now. We know who occupies the same space in the market; we know how to position ourselves differently and how to beat them.

We have taken the lead and we have created a new onebestway.

Moving from a position of feeling uncertain and sometimes afraid of taking the lead, to one of confidence and excitement, was actually quite a short journey. Arguably it wasn't a journey at all. It felt like going through 'that door' as opposed to 'this door'. It was that simple.

One door was the way you've always done it; the other door – a tiny step to the right – is more interesting and new.

There was no-one primed to give us permission to do things differently. And there was no perfect set of circumstances either.

There are always 'blockers' and obstacles of course and I chose to ignore them.

onebestway is now described as follows:

onebestway is a clever, confident and results-focused marketing and design studio. If the work we do with clients isn't uncommonly clever and of obvious and immediate value, then it simply doesn't get through.

In saying this we've made a promise to our clients and to ourselves.

Other differences include talking to each other more quickly and more openly. We have fewer systems and we get more done. We understand more about each other's jobs because we talk more and we listen better. The empathy means that we are more understanding, more supportive and more flexible.

The Naked Office was a unique and unusual experience, of course. It was not about nakedness at all. It was about going somewhere new and a little scary with a group of people that you think you know. We were going on the journey together and we saw it from each other's individual perspectives too because we listened to each other, watched each other and looked out for each other.

Looking back, 'Naked Friday' has become symbolic of this new market position and braver business approach that we have adopted for ourselves. Naked Friday was simply a destination, the same as our new onebestway. They are so similar.

New, scary and, perhaps most significant of all, is that on a practical level, at least, they are so within reach.

Removing one's clothes is something that we do every day. Easy.

Under unusual circumstances of course it can become very difficult, traumatic and frightening. And with a shift of mindset, a togetherness, a 'why not?' attitude ('why not?' is a much better question than 'why?') then things just happen.

Whatever 'it' is, we did it!

Mike Owen
Managing Director
onebestway
www.onebestway.com

SEVEN BUSINESS LESSONS FROM *THE NAKED OFFICE*

The results for onebestway have been astounding: increased customers, morale, recruitment and revenue. There are four common-sense reasons for this, and three that I did not anticipate. Perhaps you can apply these in your organization, or for yourself.

Four common-sense tips

1   Know where you want to go. Have a vision for your organization that is *understandable by a ten-year-old*. (If they can't, your customers won't.)
2   Know where you are now. *Bring the truth into the room* (stab people in the stomach, not in the back).
3   Know what you have to do to get to where you want to go. Unlock the potential of the people *you already have* by using their natural and learned strengths every day.
4   Just do it! Take action – your success comes down to what you actually do. What you, your people and your organization do, every day.

Three unexpected factors that helped onebestway's extraordinary success

5   *Have a common enemy*. In this case it was me and the prospect of Naked Friday. In your company it may be a competitor, or the prospect of going bust.
6   Treat your key projects like a TV schedule – with a 'drop dead' deadline *that cannot be extended* because the programme has to be aired.
7   *Have fun!* I often write about this, but I had completely underestimated its role over these five days. We spend so much of our lives at work – please, enjoy!

With thanks and huge respect to Mike and all at onebestway.

ACKNOWLEDGEMENTS, RESOURCES AND SUSTAINABILITY

ACKNOWLEDGEMENTS

Thank you to everyone who has helped with this one, especially Rosalind, and our two cats Mozart and Sassafras who slept through much of its writing. Thanks also to Emma Swaisland, my editor – this book was much easier to describe than to write!

RESOURCES

Please visit the people and websites mentioned throughout the book; they have all been very carefully selected.

For a full list of these, along with recommended experts, speakers and books, as well as lots of free advice, guidance and resources, please visit www.nakedleader.com.

For now, here are some books you may find useful:

Business building books

Book Yourself Solid by Michael Port
How Come THAT Idiot's Rich, and I'm Not? by Robert Shemin
Multiple Streams of Income by Robert Allen

Influence and persuasion books

Neuro-Linguistic Programming for Dummies by Romilla Ready, Kate Burton
Get Anyone to Do Anything by David J. Lieberman
Guide to Transformation by Richard Bandler

Naked Leader books

The Naked Leader
The Naked Leader Experience
The Naked Coach

SUSTAINABILITY

Please visit www.nakedleader.com – the home of leadership, to network with, share and discover actions and choices that will accelerate your journey, business and success.

Can I help you?

Email david@nakedleader.com or call 0044-1483-766502.

INDEX